THIRD edition

STRATEGIES FOR
Content Area Learning

Jerry L. Johns ● Roberta L. Berglund

D1573011

Kendall Hunt
publishing company

Book Team

Chairman and Chief Executive Officer   Mark C. Falb
President and Chief Operating Officer   Chad M. Chandlee
Vice President, Higher Education   David L. Tart
Director of Publishing Partnerships   Paul B. Carty
Editorial Manager   Georgia Botsford
Developmental Editor   Melissa Tittle
Vice President, Operations   Timothy J. Beitzel
Assistant Vice President, Production Services   Christine E. O'Brien
Senior Production Editor   Sheri Hosek
Permissions Editor   Caroline Kieler
Cover Designer   Mallory Blondin

Author Information for Correspondence and Workshops

Jerry L. Johns, Ph.D.
Consultant in Reading
E-mail: *jjohns@niu.edu*
Fax: 815-899-3022

Roberta L. Berglund, Ed.D.
Consultant in Reading/Language Arts
E-mail: *readboulder@yahoo.com*

Ordering Information

Address: Kendall Hunt Publishing Company
4050 Westmark Drive
Dubuque, IA 52004
Telephone: 800-247-3458, ext. 4
Website: www.kendallhunt.com
Fax: 800-772-9165

Kendall Hunt
publishing company

www.kendallhunt.com
Send all inquiries to:
4050 Westmark Drive
Dubuque, IA 52004-1840

Cover and title page images © Shutterstock, Inc.

Copyright © 2002, 2006, 2011 by Kendall Hunt Publishing Company

ISBN 978-0-7575-8737-5

Printed in the United States of America
10   9   8   7   6   5   4   3   2

Website Reproducibles and Content Area Samples for Selected Strategies

Preface and Overview

Who Will Use This Book?

We have written this practical and useful book for a wide range of professionals in middle and high schools, including content area teachers and those working with struggling learners. The book is ideal for school, district, and other types of professional development programs. It will also be a helpful supplement in undergraduate and graduate reading and language arts classes as well as in clinical courses where there is a desire to provide useful strategies that have wide applicability across the content areas. Professors teaching content area courses will find the book especially valuable.

What Are Some of the Outstanding Qualities of This Book?

There are several outstanding qualities of this book.

1. The book contains strategies that have utility across the curriculum.
2. The strategies are organized around three important areas: vocabulary, comprehension, and response.
3. The strategies are presented with a unique and helpful chart that quickly shows when, why, and how to use them. The type of text (narrative or informational) with which the strategy can be used is also indicated.
4. The strategies are presented in an easy-to-follow, step-by-step manner.
5. Most of the strategies contain one or more examples from the various content areas that comprise the curriculum.
6. A reproducible master accompanies most strategies.
7. A website contains extra reproducibles for many strategies, examples using various content areas, and helpful resources for instruction. Go to http://webcom3.grtxle.com/ancillary and use username JB_Content and password JB_Content for access.

What Grade Levels Do the Strategies Address?

The strategies in this book are relevant for the middle grades through high school. After reading about a strategy, it should be quite easy for you to determine how best to use it with your students. You will probably want to adapt some of the strategies to fit your teaching style, text materials, and your students' particular needs.

What Insights Have Been Provided by Research?

Gray (1925) and Herber (1970) established the importance of the relationship between literacy and learning in the content areas. Students must internalize the language of specific disciplines in order to think critically about the content. Unfortunately, studies have found that as content becomes more complex, student engagement with subject area reading declines significantly, most often by eighth grade. This drop is related to a decrease in content literacy instruction that encourages self-questioning and deep reading (Guthrie & Davis, 2003). To continue to engage older students in their content area learning, strategy instruction including the use of graphic organizers, comprehension monitoring, questioning, and summarizing are of critical importance. Students also need a variety of strategies to retain content word meanings. Such strategies include self-selecting words, making personal connections, and noting semantic relationships (Baumann, Kameenui, & Ash, 2003; Carr, 1985). Finally, opportunities to respond to text and share responses with peers through hands-on activities and discussion are effective for learning and retaining content vocabulary (Stahl & Fairbanks, 1986). The strategies in this book reflect the findings of these and other studies documenting the effectiveness of content area reading strategies (Fisher & Frey, 2008; Hedrick, Harmon, & Wood, 2008).

There is little doubt that teaching results in student learning. A persistent problem is that of teachers mentioning a skill or assigning a task without taking the time to teach it. Instruction that is characterized by clear explanation, modeling, and facilitating scaffolded practice can increase student learning. The National Reading Panel (2000) compiled a large volume that offers several strategies for effective comprehension instruction. According to Cunningham (2001), the comprehension section of the report is potentially valuable. The following principles are generally consistent with two other major reviews (Pearson & Fielding, 1991; Tierney & Cunningham, 1984) and a related chapter (Pressley, 2000) of research on teaching comprehension.

1. Teach students to be aware of their own comprehension. This strategy is often referred to as comprehension monitoring.
2. Have students work together on their strategies. This strategy is called cooperative learning.
3. Have students make graphic summaries of what is read through the use of graphic and semantic organizers. Use them as a bridge to student-generated talk or writing.
4. Use story and text structure.
5. Help students learn to ask and answer questions.
6. Teach students to summarize what is read.

The strategies selected for this book will help you in each of these areas. The key ingredients, however, are your actions as the teacher. Consider the following model.

- Take time to teach the strategies.

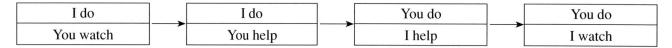

- Tell students how the strategies promote learning.
- Model how the strategies are used.
- Think aloud by describing what goes on in your mind as you are using the strategy.
- Gradually release the responsibility to students.
- Provide guided practice so students can learn how the strategy will help them understand the lesson or text.
- Reinforce their efforts.
- Develop the strategies over time and remind students to use their strategies in a variety of contexts.
- Have students reflect on the strategies and how they help in particular contexts.

Finally, we want to stress again the critical importance of teaching the strategies.

Is This Book Easy to Use?

Yes! The format and organization of this book makes it very user friendly. We have also included a Quick Reference Guide inside the front cover so you can quickly locate the various strategies and consider their use. Note that the strategies are listed in alphabetical order. There is also a reference page on the back cover.

Where Should I Begin?

Glance at the Quick Reference Guide inside the front cover. Scan the strategies and find a particular strategy that interests you. Turn to the page for that strategy. Suppose you select the Discussion Web on page 27. Under the title, you will see a chart that covers five areas.

1. **FOCUS** indicates how many of the three areas (i.e., vocabulary, comprehension, and response) are covered by the strategy. The Discussion Web focuses on *comprehension* and *response*. Response indicates that oral or written actions by students are part of this strategy.

2. **TEXT TYPE** refers to the two major classifications of materials: narrative and informational. The Discussion Web can be used with both types of text.

3. **WHEN TO USE** tells you if you should use the strategy before, during, and/or after reading. The Discussion Web is best used *after* reading.

4. **STRATEGY** is based on the work of Duke and Pearson (2002), Keene (2008), Keene and Zimmermann (1997), Pearson, Roehler, Dole, and Duffy (1992) and others who have conducted and reviewed the research in comprehension. These strategies help students become thoughtful, independent readers who are engaged in their reading and learning. The following are brief descriptions of the seven major strategies we use in this book.

   - *Monitoring Meaning*—Students who monitor meaning as they read know if the text makes sense to them. If not, they use fix-up strategies such as pausing, rereading, and/or discussing their understanding with others to help clarify the meaning.

   - *Using Relevant Prior Knowledge*—Students use their background knowledge before, during, and after reading to make sense of and remember new information. They assimilate new information into their background knowledge. This is sometimes referred to as using and developing their schema.

   - *Asking Questions*—Students generate questions before, during, and after reading. They use their questions to help them focus and remember important ideas from the text.

   - *Inferring*—Students combine their prior knowledge with that which is read to create meaning that is not explicitly stated in the text. Readers who infer draw conclusions, make and revise predictions, use and interpret information from the text, make connections, answer questions, and make judgments about the reading.

   - *Creating Images*—Using all five senses and their emotions, students create images during and after reading. They may use their images to make connections, recall, and interpret details from the reading.

   - *Determining Importance*—As they read, students make decisions about what they believe is important in the text. These might be words, sentences, or main ideas developed from the reading. They then draw conclusions about the key ideas or major concepts contained in the text.

   - *Synthesizing*—Students put together information from the text, from other relevant sources, and their background knowledge to create understanding of what has been read. Students use text structures and text elements as they read to predict, confirm or reject ideas, assimilate thoughts and create overall meaning. "A synthesis is the sum of information from the text, other relevant texts, and the reader's background knowledge . . . produced in an original way" (Keene, 2008, p. 252).

   You can see that the Discussion Web helps with *inferring, determining importance*, and *synthesizing*.

5. **HOW TO USE** refers to whether the strategy is best used with individuals, small groups, and/or whole groups. You can see that the Discussion Web is best used with *small groups* and *whole groups*. There is amazing variety in how the strategies can be used, so don't be limited by our recommendations. You'll likely find additional ways to use the strategies that increase student engagement.

Below the title of the strategy are the words *Description* and *Procedure*. There is a brief description of the Discussion Web followed by a step-by-step procedure for using it. We like to think of the numbered steps as a systematic lesson plan to help you present the strategy to your students. You should, of course, feel free to adapt the steps and examples to fit your students.

We then provide one or more *examples* (see page vii) of how the strategy might be used in different subjects or content areas. You may quickly be able to think of logical extensions to your lessons in a variety of areas.

Focus
Comprehension
Response

Text Type
Narrative
Informational

When to Use
After Reading

Strategy
Inferring
Determining Importance
Synthesizing

How to Use
Small Group
Whole Group

Discussion Web

DESCRIPTION: The Discussion Web (Alvermann, 1991; Duthie, 1986) is a graphic aid for helping students address both sides of an issue by considering pro and con arguments before drawing a conclusion. Active discussion is stimulated by this strategy, which incorporates reading, speaking, listening, and writing.

Text Type
Narrative
Informational

When to Use
After Reading

Procedure

1. Choose a selection that has the potential to generate opposing viewpoints. Be sure to initially develop an understanding of key vocabulary, survey illustrations and charts, build background knowledge as needed, and help students set purposes for reading. Then have students read the selection.

2. Display the reproducible master on page 30 and duplicate and distribute copies to students. To introduce the Discussion Web, pose a question related to the selection that stimulates opposing views. Have students write the question on their Discussion Web.

3. Have students work with a partner to brainstorm at least three responses for each side of the question posed. Encourage students to write down key words or phrases and strive to have an equal number of reasons in each column. Students could take turns writing reasons on the same Discussion Web. Provide ample time for each set of partners to share their reasons.

4. Pair one set of partners with another set of partners so they can compare their reasons. Tell the groups that the goal is to work toward consensus. Provide time for students to share and discuss. Encourage students to listen carefully, especially for views that may differ from their own. The conclusion can be written in the box on the bottom of the sheet.

5. Select or have each group select an individual to serve as a group spokesperson. Provide three to five minutes for each group to decide which of the group's reasons best support the group's conclusion and check or star the best reasons. Then have the spokesperson from each group report to the whole class.

6. If desired, invite students to write their individual answers to the question posed on the Discussion Web.

7. Consider the following variations of the Discussion Web based on Alvermann (1991) and Swafford (1990).

   - Current or historical issues can be explored by making simple changes in the Discussion Web. The U.S. Civil War slavery issue could be examined through the positions of Stephen A. Douglas and Abraham Lincoln. A partial Discussion Web showing this example follows.

Strategy
Inferring
Determining Importance
Synthesizing

How to Use
Small Group
Whole Group

To make the strategy especially useful, a *reproducible master* is included for most of the strategies. You have the publisher's permission to reproduce and use the master with your students within the guidelines noted on the copyright page of this book.

References

Baumann, J. F., Kameenui, E. J., & Ash, G. E. (2003). Research on vocabulary instruction: Voltaire redux. In J. Flood, D. Lapp, J. R. Squire, & J. M. Jenson (Eds.), *Handbook on teaching the English language arts* (pp. 752–785). Mahwah, NJ: Erlbaum.

Carr, E. M. (1985). The vocabulary overview guide: A metacognitive strategy to improve vocabulary comprehension and retention. *Journal of Reading, 28*, 684–689.

Cunningham, J. W. (2001). The National Reading Panel Report (Essay Book Review). *Reading Research Quarterly, 36*, 326–335.

Duke, N., & Pearson, P. D. (2002). Effective practices for developing reading comprehension. In A. E. Farstrup & S. J. Samuels (Eds.), *What research has to say about reading instruction* (3rd ed.) (pp. 205–242). Newark, DE: International Reading Association. (2001). The National Reading Panel Report (Essay Book Review). *Reading Research Quarterly, 36*, 326–335.

Fisher, D., & Frey, N. (2008). Student and teacher perspectives on the usefulness of content literacy strategies. *Literacy Research and Instruction, 47*, 246–263.

Gray, W. S. (1925). Reading activities in school and in social life. In G. M. Whipple (Ed.), *The Twenty-fourth yearbook of the national society for the study of education, Part I* (pp. 1–8). Bloomington, IL: Public School Publishing.

Guthrie, J. T., & Davis, M. H. (2003). Motivating struggling readers in middle school through an engagement model of classroom practice. *Reading & Writing Quarterly, 19*, 59–85.

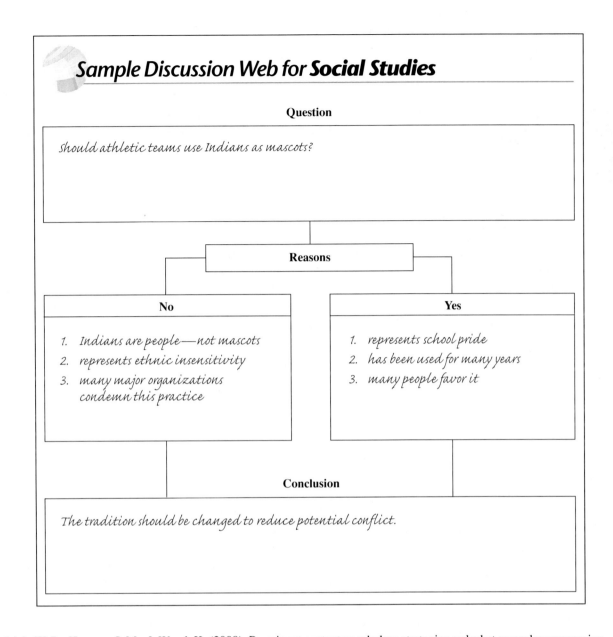

Sample Discussion Web for *Social Studies*

Question

Should athletic teams use Indians as mascots?

Reasons

No	**Yes**
1. *Indians are people—not mascots* 2. *represents ethnic insensitivity* 3. *many major organizations condemn this practice*	1. *represents school pride* 2. *has been used for many years* 3. *many people favor it*

Conclusion

The tradition should be changed to reduce potential conflict.

Hedrick, W. R., Harmon, J. M., & Wood, K. (2008). Prominent content vocabulary strategies and what secondary preservice teachers think about them. *Reading Psychology, 29,* 443–470.

Herber, H. L. (1970). *Teaching reading in content areas.* Englewood Cliffs, NJ: Prentice-Hall.

Keene, E. O. (2008). *To understand: New horizons in reading comprehension.* Portsmouth, NH: Heinemann.

Keene, E. O., & Zimmermann, S. (1997). *Mosaic of thought.* Portsmouth, NH: Heinemann.

National Reading Panel. (2000). *Teaching children to read: An evidence-based assessment of the scientific research literature on reading and its implications for reading instruction.* Washington, DC: National Institute for Child Health & Human Development.

Pearson, P. D., & Fielding, L. (1991). Comprehension instruction. In R. Barr, M. L. Kamil, P. B. Mosenthal, & P. D. Pearson (Eds.), *Handbook of reading research* (Vol. II) (pp. 815–816). White Plains, NY: Longman.

Pearson, P. D., Roehler, L. R., Dole, J. A., & Duffy, G. G. (1992). Developing expertise in reading comprehension. In S. J. Samuels & A. E. Farstrup (Eds.), *What research has to say about reading instruction* (2nd ed.) (pp. 145–199). Newark, DE: International Reading Association.

Pressley, M. (2000). What should comprehension instruction be the instruction of? In M. L. Kamil, P. B. Mosenthal, P. D. Pearson, & R. Barr (Eds.), *Handbook of reading research* (Vol. III) (pp. 545–561). Mahwah, NJ: Erlbaum.

Stahl, S. A., & Fairbanks, M. (1986). The effects of vocabulary instruction: A model-based meta-analysis. *Review of Educational Research, 56,* 72–110.

Tierney, R. J., & Cunningham, J. W. (1984). Research on teaching reading comprehension. In P. D. Pearson, R. Barr, M. L. Kamil, & P. Mosenthal (Eds.), *Handbook of reading research* (Vol. I) (pp. 609–655). White Plains, NY: Longman.

About the Authors

Jerry L. Johns has been recognized as a distinguished teacher, writer, outstanding teacher educator, and popular professional development speaker for schools, school districts, and conferences. His more than 700 presentations have involved travel throughout the United States and 13 countries. He has taught students from kindergarten through graduate school and also served as a reading teacher. Professor Johns spent his career at Northern Illinois University. He was also a Visiting Professor at Western Washington University and the University of Victoria in British Columbia.

Professor Johns served in leadership positions at the local, state, national, and international levels. He has been president of the International Reading Association, the Illinois Reading Council, the Association of Literacy Educators and Researchers, and the Northern Illinois Reading Council. He also served on the Board of Directors for each of these organizations as well as the American Reading Forum. In addition, Dr. Johns has served on numerous committees of the International Reading Association and other professional organizations.

Dr. Johns has authored or coauthored nearly 300 articles, monographs, and research studies as well as numerous professional books. His *Basic Reading Inventory*, now in the tenth edition, is widely used in undergraduate and graduate classes as well as by practicing teachers. Among his more than 20 coauthored books to help teachers strengthen their reading instruction are *Improving Reading: Interventions, Strategies, and Resources, Teaching Reading Pre-K–Grade 3, Essential Comprehension Strategies for the Intermediate Grades, Spanish Reading Inventory, Comprehension and Vocabulary Strategies for the Elementary Grades,* and *Reading and Learning Strategies: Middle Grades through High School.* Professor Johns currently serves on the editorial advisory boards for *Reading Psychology* and the *Illinois Reading Council Journal.*

Dr. Johns has been the recipient of numerous awards for his contributions to the profession. The Illinois Reading Council honored him with the induction into the Reading Hall of Fame. Other recognitions include the Alpha Delta Literacy Award for Scholarship, Leadership, and Service to Adult Learners and the A.B. Herr Award for outstanding contributions to the field of reading. He also received the Outstanding Teacher Educator in Reading Award presented by the International Reading Association, the Champion for Children Award presented by the HOSTS Corporation, and the Laureate Award from the Association of Literacy Educators and Researchers for life-long contributors to the field of reading.

Roberta L. (Bobbi) Berglund has had a long and distinguished career in education. Her public school experience spans more than thirty years and includes serving as a classroom teacher, reading specialist, Title I Director, and district curriculum administrator. For several years, Dr. Berglund was a member of the reading faculty at the University of Wisconsin-Whitewater where she taught graduate and undergraduate reading courses and worked with student teachers. She has also taught graduate reading courses at several other colleges and universities including Northern Illinois University, Rockford College, National-Louis University, and Aurora University. Dr. Berglund has served as a consultant in the area of reading, working with school districts and cooperative education services in developing curriculum and assessments, conducting staff development, and guiding the selection of instructional materials. She is currently working with Response to Intervention initiatives as well as planning and implementing effective reading instruction for English Language Learners (ELLs) in the elementary grades. She recently received a grant to refine the use of evidence-based vocabulary and comprehension strategies to assist ELLs in accessing and reading informational text.

Dr. Berglund has received honors for outstanding service to several organizations and has been selected as a member of the Illinois Reading Council Hall of Fame. She was also honored with the Those Who Excel Award from the Illinois State Board of Education. She has served on several committees of the International Reading Association (IRA) including the Program Committees for the Annual Convention and the World Congress in Scotland. She has also chaired the Publications Committee which provided leadership for four professional journals, a newspaper, and the development of professional books. She provided leadership in the conceptualization and establishment of a free, internet-based source of high-quality practices and resources in reading and language arts instruction. Dr. Berglund has also served as the editor of a professional journal and has been on the editorial advisory boards for several others.

Dr. Berglund conducts workshops for teachers and administrators and has been invited to make presentations at state, national, and international conferences. She is the author of over fifty publications and is the author or coauthor of fourteen professional books including *Strategies for Content Area Learning: Vocabulary, Comprehension, and Response, Essential Comprehension Strategies for the Intermediate Grades,* and *Fluency: Differentiated Interventions and Progress-Monitoring Assessments.*

Anticipation/Reaction Guide

DESCRIPTION: The Anticipation/Reaction Guide (Herber, 1978) is a series of statements about a selection. If the statements serve as an Anticipation Guide, students' thoughts and opinions are sought prior to reading the selection. If the statements serve as a Reaction Guide, students evaluate the statements in relationship to the selection they have read. Using the statements before and after reading would be an Anticipation/Reaction Guide, and students respond to the statements prior to and after reading.

Procedure

1. Decide which variation of the Anticipation/Reaction Guide you will use. The strategy is commonly used with informational materials, but it can also be used with narrative materials. See page 2 for a sample guide for science.

2. Identify the major ideas or concepts in the materials and create five to seven statements related to them. Try to create statements that challenge or support students' preconceived notions related to the major ideas or concepts in the materials to be read.

3. Write the statements on the Anticipation/Reaction Guide reproducible master on page 3, duplicate it, and distribute it to students. The remaining steps in this section describe how to present an Anticipation/Reaction Guide.

4. Distribute a copy of the Anticipation/Reaction Guide to each student. For instructional purposes, you may also want to display a copy of the guide distributed to students.

5. Direct students' attention to the statements on the guide and have them look at the Before Reading column. Tell them that they should read the statements and check those with which they agree prior to reading the selection. Ask them if the statements remind them of something they already know about.

6. After students have completed the Before Reading column, have them discuss the statements. The discussion could take place in small groups or with the whole class. Then have students read the selection upon which the statements are based.

7. After students have read the selection, they should complete the After Reading column. Stress that students should base their responses in the After Reading column on information from the selection. Ask students how the connections or questions they made prior to reading helped them to better understand the selection.

8. Engage students in a follow-up discussion to determine whether their ideas have changed and why. Encourage students to use information from the selection to support their ideas. Help students understand that it is common for their ideas to change as a result of reading and discussing the selection.

Focus
Comprehension
Response

Text Type
Narrative
Informational

When to Use
Before Reading
After Reading

Strategy
Monitoring Meaning
Using Prior Knowledge
Asking Questions
Inferring
Determining Importance

How to Use
Individual
Whole Group

9. Seek ways to use the guides on the website with a variety of reading selections. Consider using variety in the words for the columns that students check. Possible words are provided below.

Before Reading	After Reading
Agree	Disagree
Tend to Agree	Tend to Disagree
True	False
Likely	Unlikely
Yes	No
Fact	Opinion

10. An alternative approach is to have students complete the Before Reading column independently. Then designate one side of the room "Agree" and the other side of the room "Disagree." After each statement is read aloud, have students move about the room to indicate whether they agree or disagree. Invite discussion and interaction.

11. See the website for additional reproducibles.

Reference

Herber, H. L. (1978). *Teaching reading in content areas* (2nd ed.). Upper Saddle River, NJ: Prentice Hall.

Sample Anticipation Guide for Science

Directions: Before you read the booklet *Summer Health Guide*, read the statements below and check those with which you agree. We will then discuss the statements.

Before Reading

Agree	Disagree	
	✓	1. Experts say even one bad sunburn during childhood or teenage years can double your risk of getting skin cancer as an adult.
✓		2. Gray, green, and brown sunglass lenses are the best.
	✓	3. A wet T-shirt can protect you from getting sunburned.
✓		4. The best time to apply sunscreen is when you first go out into the sun.
	✓	5. If your sunscreen has an SPF (sun protection factor) of 10, that means you can stay out in the sun for 10 hours.
✓		6. The sun's rays can damage your vision over time.
✓		7. The more you pay for sunglasses, the better they protect your eyes.
	✓	8. Skin cancer is the fastest growing type of cancer.
	✓	9. If you are taking medication for acne, an infection, or birth control, your skin and eyes can be more sensitive to the sun's rays.
✓		10. The darker the sunglass lenses, the more protection you get from the sun's ultraviolet rays.
✓		11. Nonwhite teens don't need to use sunscreen.
✓		12. Sunglasses with polarizing lenses are best for skiing and water sports.

Anticipation/Reaction Guide

Title _____

☐ **Anticipation Guide**
Before Reading

☐ **Reaction Guide**
After Reading

Agree	Disagree		Agree	Disagree
_____	_____	1.	_____	_____
_____	_____	2.	_____	_____
_____	_____	3.	_____	_____
_____	_____	4.	_____	_____
_____	_____	5.	_____	_____
_____	_____	6.	_____	_____
_____	_____	7.	_____	_____

Before-During-After (B-D-A)

DESCRIPTION: The Before-During-After (B-D-A) strategy (Laverick, 2002) is an adaptation of the well-established and popular K-W-L strategy (Ogle, 1986). B-D-A focuses on the essential components of effective reading and encourages students to use the proficient reader strategies of predicting, focusing, note taking, summarizing, and determining the main idea before, during, and after reading. Laverick developed the B-D-A strategy to provide guidance to adolescents in helping them to focus on and internalize information from text.

Procedure

1. Duplicate copies of the B-D-A reproducible master on page 7 and distribute them to students.

2. Before reading, invite students to brainstorm and list what is known about the topic to be studied. This can be done individually, with partners, or as a whole group. The brainstormed ideas should be listed under the "Before" column on the strategy form.

3. Explain to students that as they read the selection, they need to note new information under the "During" column. This can be done individually, with partners, or in small groups. Tell students that they need to put a plus (+) next to statements in the "Before" column if they are found to be correct.

4. When students finish reading, invite them to briefly summarize the information under the "After" column. Students can share their summaries in small groups or with the whole class.

5. When students have shared and possibly revised their summaries, have them review the information in the "Before" column. Note those items that were found to be accurate. Discuss with students how they might determine the accuracy of ideas shared that weren't confirmed or disconfirmed by the reading.

6. Instruct students to develop three questions and write them in the "After" column. These questions should be those that could be answered by students who have read the text. If students have worked with Question-Answer Relationships (see page 91), you may want to have them develop questions in each of the QAR categories. If the answers to the questions can be located in a specific place in the text, have students note the page number next to the question. A sample completed B-D-A is found on page 6.

7. In small- or whole-group discussion, students should share their questions and invite their classmates to answer them.

8. Finally, work with the whole class to develop a one-sentence main idea.

References

Laverick, C. (2002). B-D-A strategy: Reinventing the wheel can be a good thing. *Journal of Adolescent and Adult Literacy, 46*, 144–147.

Ogle, D. (1986). K-W-L: A teaching model that develops active reading of expository text. *The Reading Teacher, 39*, 564–570.

Focus
Comprehension

Text Type
Informational

When to Use
Before Reading
During Reading
After Reading

Strategy
Using Prior Knowledge
Asking Questions
Inferring
Determining Importance

How to Use
Individual
Small Group
Whole Group

Before-During-After (B-D-A)

Title _Greece_

Before	During	After
What I Think I Know About This Topic	What's New	My Summary and Three Questions

+ - Europe
 	
+ - center of ancient civilization
 	
+ - Athens—capital
 	
+ - windmills
 	
+ - Parthenon
  - home of Olympic games
  - larger than Italy
	- part of Balkan Peninsula
	
	- major industries
	  - tourism
	  - shipping
	  - oil refining
	  - food stuffs
	
	- earthquake prone
	
	- many islands
	
	- Greek Orthodox religion
	
	- Euro is currency
	
	- people speak Greek
		This was about . . .
		
		Greece is a small European country whose history has influenced much of the Western World. It is a diverse land of urban and rural, mountains and seacoast, old world and modern cultures.
		
		1. _How has ancient Greece influenced us today?_
		
		2. _What is the capital city? (p. 116)_
		
		3. _What might a visitor to Greece expect to see?_

Here's the main idea in one sentence: _This selection provided basic information about Greece._

Before-During-After (B-D-A)

Title _____

Before	During	After
What I Think I Know About This Topic	What's New	My Summary and Three Questions
		This was about . . .
		1.
		2.
		3.

Here's the main idea in one sentence: _____

_____

_____

Bookmarks

DESCRIPTION: Bookmarks (Beers, 2003; Daniels & Zemelman, 2004) give students a place to record brief thoughts while reading. When students record their thoughts on the Bookmarks, they become active readers who make connections, ask questions, and determine important ideas. Bookmarks can also be used for recording key concepts or vocabulary words that are significant to the reading.

Procedure

1. Duplicate and distribute copies of the Bookmarks reproducible master on page 11. Have students fold the reproducible in half (vertically).

2. Select an excerpt from a text that your students will be asked to read.

3. Read a portion of the text aloud and model what kinds of thoughts can be recorded on Bookmarks. Try to provide examples that include a variety of responses: personal connections, questions, important passages, and key vocabulary.

4. Have students continue reading from the text and record their thoughts on the Bookmarks as they read. A completed sample is found on page 10.

5. Invite students to discuss their responses with a partner or in collaborative groups.

6. Encourage whole group sharing to identify the variety of responses students recorded while reading.

7. Bookmarks can also be used after reading to help students recall their understanding of the selected text.

References

Beers, K. (2003). *When kids can't read: What teachers can do.* Portsmouth, NH: Heinemann.

Daniels, H., & Zemelman, S. (2004). *Subjects matter: Every teacher's guide to content-area reading.* Portsmouth, NH: Heinemann.

Focus
Vocabulary
Comprehension
Response

Text Type
Narrative
Informational

When to Use
During Reading

Strategy
Monitoring Meaning
Using Prior Knowledge
Asking Questions
Inferring
Determining Importance
Synthesizing

How to Use
Individual

Name: _Amy_

Topic: _Louisiana Purchase_

— Robert Livingston and James Monroe negotiated the purchase.

— What would have happened if Napoleon decided not to sell the Louisiana Territory?

— I think at the time, $15 million was a lot of money for the purchase. The aftermath of Hurricane Katrina will cost much more.

— How much land did the U.S. actually acquire?

— I now understand how the "French Quarter" in New Orleans got its name.

— How much money did the federal government give Lewis and Clark for their expedition?

Name: _Amy_

Topic: _Louisiana Purchase_

Vocabulary Word: _cede_

Page _362_

to grant or give up land

Vocabulary Word: _Louisiana Territory_

Page _362_

Land from the Mississippi River west to the Rocky Mountains

Vocabulary Word: _constructionists_

Page _363_

those who believed that the federal government can only do what the Constitution says, nothing more

Vocabulary Word: _envoy_

Page _363_

a diplomat sent to negotiate the purchase

Vocabulary Word: _____

Page _____

Bookmarks

Name: _____

Topic: _____

Name: _____

Topic: _____

Vocabulary Word: _____

Page _____

Vocabulary Word: _____

Page _____

Vocabulary Word: _____

Page _____

Vocabulary Word: _____

Page _____

Vocabulary Word: _____

Page _____

Character Feelings and Traits

Focus
Comprehension
Response

Text Type
Narrative
Informational

When to Use
After Reading

Strategy
Using Prior Knowledge
Inferring
Creating Images
Determining Importance
Synthesizing

How to Use
Individual
Small Group
Whole Group

DESCRIPTION: Character Feelings and Traits (Johns & Lenski, 2010) can be used with fictional characters and historical or living individuals. Students are asked to identify feelings or traits (or both) of fictional and real individuals and offer support for the feelings and traits identified through an analysis of printed materials (e.g., a story, a section of text, a newspaper article, or historical documents).

Procedure

1. Write the words *feelings* and *traits* on the board. Help students understand that *feelings* are emotions, sentiments, or desires and that *traits* are distinguishing features of the character or individual.

2. Have students work individually, with a partner, or in small groups to identify specific feelings and traits. After about three minutes, have students share their words and write them under the proper category. A partial example is shown below. A more complete list of Character Traits is available on the website.

Feelings	Traits
happy	honest
pleased	hard working
anxious	dishonest
nervous	creative

3. Help students understand that some words may characterize both feelings and traits. For example, nervous is usually a feeling, but it could also be a trait that characterizes a particular individual.

4. Identify a reading selection (narrative or informational) for which the Character Feelings and Traits reproducible masters (pages 15–16) would be appropriate. Decide if you will use feelings, traits, or both.

5. After reading, have students write the name of the individual in the oval. Then have students review the selection and decide upon some feelings and/or traits. These words can be written on the arrowed line. Students should then support the words they chose with information from the selection.

6. Provide time for students to discuss their responses in small groups. If there are several characters in a story or play, students might select one of the characters and complete the sheet. Small groups of students could then share their thoughts about the same characters. If a current or historical individual is the focus of the selection, a whole group discussion could be used.

Reference

Johns, J. L., & Lenski, S. D. (2010). *Improving reading: Interventions, strategies, and resources* (5th ed.). Dubuque, IA: Kendall Hunt.

Sample Character Feelings for Middle School Language Arts

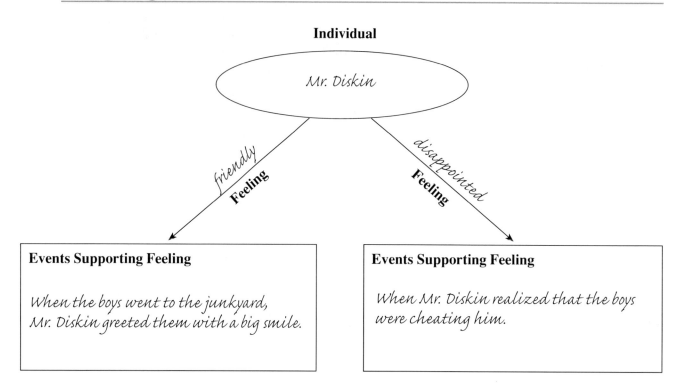

Individual

Mr. Diskin

friendly **Feeling**

disappointed **Feeling**

Events Supporting Feeling

When the boys went to the junkyard, Mr. Diskin greeted them with a big smile.

Events Supporting Feeling

When Mr. Diskin realized that the boys were cheating him.

*Sample Character Traits for **Social Studies***

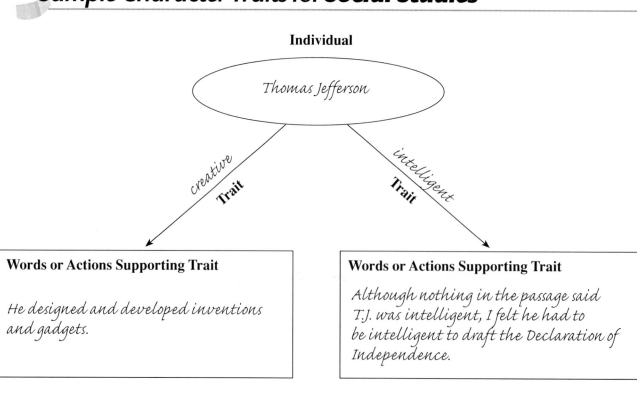

Individual

Thomas Jefferson

creative **Trait**

intelligent **Trait**

Words or Actions Supporting Trait

He designed and developed inventions and gadgets.

Words or Actions Supporting Trait

Although nothing in the passage said T.J. was intelligent, I felt he had to be intelligent to draft the Declaration of Independence.

Character Feelings

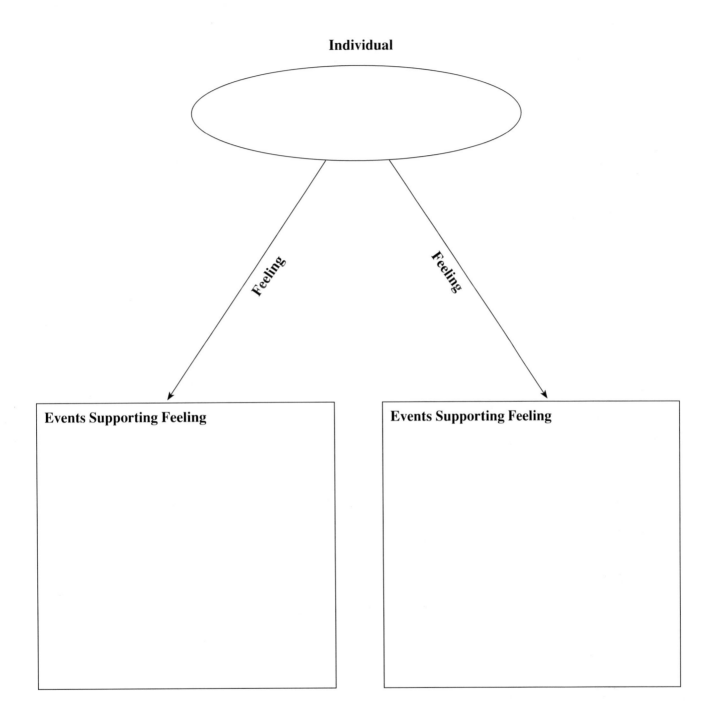

Individual

Feeling

Feeling

Events Supporting Feeling

Events Supporting Feeling

Character Traits

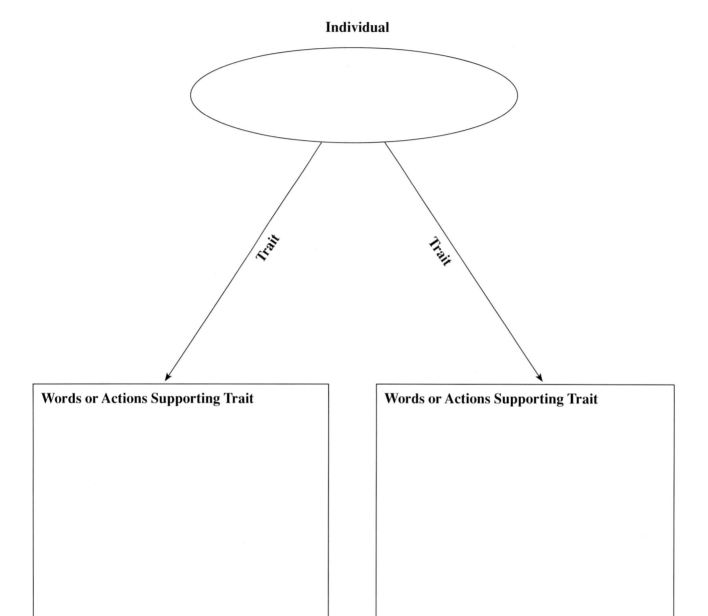

Individual

Trait

Trait

Words or Actions Supporting Trait

Words or Actions Supporting Trait

Concept Circles

Focus
Vocabulary
Comprehension

Text Type
Narrative
Informational

When to Use
After Reading

Strategy
Using Prior Knowledge
Asking Questions
Inferring
Determining Importance
Synthesizing

How to Use
Individual
Small Group

DESCRIPTION: Concept Circles (Vacca, Vacca, & Mraz, 2011) provide opportunities for students to study words and relate them to one another. Concept Circles are intriguing to students as they categorize words in a visual way rather than in lists. This strategy is often viewed by students as "fun" while providing an opportunity for them to extend their understanding of concept words. There are three ways to work with Concept Circles. The first asks students to view a completed circle containing four words or phrases and to identify the concept represented by all of the words or phrases in the circle. In a second pattern, one or two of the quadrants are left empty and students are invited to add words to fit the concept as well as name it. The third way of using Concept Circles is to identify the word or phrase in the circle that does not relate to the others, cross it out, and then identify the concept that exists among the remaining sections. Students could also be asked to replace the crossed-out word or phrase with one that fits the concept. All of the ways of working with Concept Circles involve students in thinking about how words relate to each other and how they relate to a superordinate concept. Concept Circles can serve as a quick and meaningful review of major concepts. Concept Circles also work well as an in-class activity, as a homework assignment, or as a means of assessing student understanding of major ideas and relationships.

Procedure

1. Make copies of the Concept Circles graphic organizers on pages 20–22 and display them. Tell students that this type of graphic can help them think about some of the central concepts in their lesson or unit of study.

2. Model the use of Concept Circles by choosing well-understood concepts and inviting the class to participate in completing the circles with you. For example, the words in the circle might be *Pilot, Navigator, Escalade*, and *RAV4*. Ask students, "What word or phrase could you use to identify the concept that would include all of these words?" Students might suggest *automobiles, trucks*, or *sport utility vehicles*. Write the category they select on the line above the circle. Next, show another circle where the words included might be *steering wheel, visor, seats*. Ask, "What is the concept?" Students might say, "parts of cars" or "auto interiors." Write one of the responses on the line at the top of the Concept Circle. Next ask, "What word could you add to our circle that fits the concept?" Students might suggest *seat belts, carpet*, or *odometer*. Choose one and write it in the blank quadrant of the circle. Finally, show students a completed circle in which one of the words included in the circle does not fit the concept. Have the students read the four words in the circle. Then tell them, "All but one relate to which concept." An example might be *Ford, Chevrolet, Chrysler, Sony*. Then say, "One of the words doesn't belong. Can you identify it and tell us why you chose it?" After students identify *Sony* as the word that doesn't fit, cross out that word. Then ask students to identify the concept "cars" or "autos" and ask them to suggest a replacement for *Sony* that fits the concept. Students might suggest *Honda* or *Toyota*. Write the new word in the quadrant.

3. After modeling, give students an opportunity to complete Concept Circles independently. You may want to invite students to work individually or in pairs to complete Concept Circle activities you have developed, or have them use the reproducible masters on pages 20–22 to create circles using words from the lesson or unit of study.

4. When the circles are completed, have students share some of their ideas and present them to the rest of the class. Their peers will enjoy matching wits with the circles' creators by guessing the superordinate concepts, suggesting other words that might relate to the concept, or reviewing the words that don't "fit" the identified concept.

Reference

Vacca, R. T., Vacca, J. L., & Mraz, M. (2011). *Content area reading: Literacy and learning across the curriculum* (10th ed.). Boston: Pearson.

$$\underline{\quad Geologic\ Time \quad}$$
(topic)

Directions: Read the words in each circle. Determine the concept that includes all of the words or phrases in the circle. Write it on the line above the circle.

[Geologic Eras]*

[Geologic Periods]*

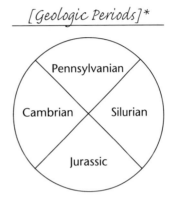

Directions: Read the words in each circle. Think of a concept that includes the words in the circle and then add a word or phrase to the circle that fits the concept. Write the appropriate concept on the line above each circle.

[Paleozoic Period]*

[Triassic Period]*

Directions: Read the words in each circle. Determine a concept that includes all but one of the words or phrases in the circle. Write the name of the concept on the line above the circle. Replace the word or phrase that doesn't fit with a better choice. Be prepared to defend your answers.

[Cretaceous Period]*

[Pennsylvanian Period]*

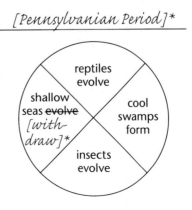

*Words in brackets [ ] indicate possible student responses.

19

Concept Circles

_____
(topic)

Directions: Read the words in each circle. Determine the concept that includes all of the words or phrases in the circle. Write it on the line above the circle.

_____

_____

_____

_____

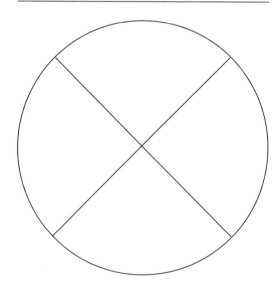

NAME _____ DATE _____

Concept Circles

_____
(topic)

Directions: Read the words in each circle. Think of a concept that includes the words in the circle and then add a word or phrase to the circle that fits the concept. Write the appropriate concept on the line above each circle.

_____   _____

_____   _____

   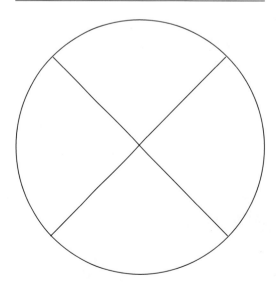

NAME _____   DATE _____

Concept Circles

_____
(topic)

Directions: Read the words in each circle. Determine a concept that includes all but one of the words or phrases in the circle. Write the name of the concept on the line above the circle. Replace the word or phrase that doesn't fit with a better choice. Be prepared to defend your answers.

_____

_____

_____

_____

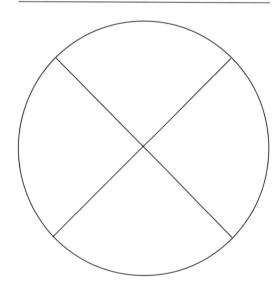

Concept Mapping

DESCRIPTION: Concept Mapping (Novak, 1991) is a technique for visualizing relationships between concepts. Concept Maps are similar to semantic maps (Heimlich & Pittelman, 1986) in that they show the structure of information in graphic form. Concept Maps are diagrams that explicitly identify major and subordinate concepts of a topic and often include labels showing how the concepts are related. Concept Maps are most often used with informational text, are especially useful in science, and are often individually designed to fit the ideas. They can be used as an advance organizer before reading to help students understand the structure of the information they will be studying. Concept Maps can also be used as a study and note-taking guide during reading where students are provided with the major concepts and asked to identify and map the related subordinate concepts as they read. Most often, however, Concept Maps are used at the culmination of a unit of study to show, in a graphic way, a synthesis of the information that has been learned. Concept Maps can be useful study tools for students and can also be used as a means of assessing student learning (Rafferty & Fleschner, 1993).

Focus
Comprehension

Text Type
Narrative
Informational

When to Use
Before Reading
During Reading
After Reading

Strategy
Determining Importance
Synthesizing

How to Use
Individual
Small Group
Whole Group

Procedure

1. Identify the major concepts of the topic being studied and select an appropriate Concept Map from page 25, the website, or create one to fit your purposes.
2. Make and display an enlarged version of the map.
3. Provide copies of the map to students.
4. Explain to students that they are going to be developing Concept Maps in order to review their work with a specific topic or subject, for example, in a study of the Digestive System, the function of the stomach.
5. Write Stomach Wall in the box at the top of the Hierarchy Concept Map and invite students to do the same on their maps.
6. Ask students to review the text information related to the topic and suggest the major concepts that they believe should be included on the map. Often, chapter headings and subheadings can be used to generate the list.
7. Next, work with students to organize the list from the most general or abstract to the most specific.
8. From the list, select the major concepts and have students write them in the appropriate spaces on the Concept Map.
9. Invite students to work individually or in pairs to add details to one or more of the central concepts on the map.
10. After students have finished their work, have them share the information from their maps and add the ideas to the enlarged map.
11. Review with students how the concepts are connected and the relationships among the ideas represented on the Concept Maps. Remind them that they can use their maps to help them remember and use the information in the chapter or unit.
12. Additional reproducibles can be found on the website.

References

Heimlich, J. E., & Pittelman, S. D. (1986). *Semantic mapping: Classroom applications.* Newark, DE: International Reading Association.

Novak, J. D. (1991). Classify with concept maps: A tool for students and teachers alike. *The Science Teacher, 58,* 45–49.

Rafferty, C. D., & Fleschner, L. K. (1993). Concept mapping: A viable alternative to objective essay exams. *Reading Research Quarterly, 32,* 25–34.

Sample Hierarchy Concept Map for **Science**

Digestion in Stomach

Hierarchy Concept Map

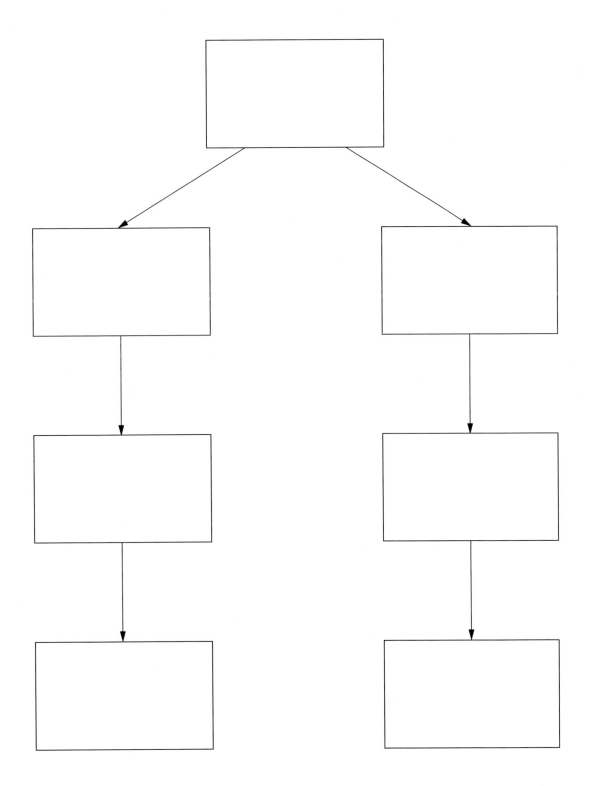

Discussion Web

DESCRIPTION: The Discussion Web (Alvermann, 1991; Duthie, 1986) is a graphic aid for helping students address both sides of an issue by considering pro and con arguments before drawing a conclusion. Active discussion is stimulated by this strategy, which incorporates reading, speaking, listening, and writing.

Procedure

1. Choose a selection that has the potential to generate opposing viewpoints. Be sure to initially develop an understanding of key vocabulary, survey illustrations and charts, build background knowledge as needed, and help students set purposes for reading. Then have students read the selection.

2. Display the reproducible master on page 30 and duplicate and distribute copies to students. To introduce the Discussion Web, pose a question related to the selection that stimulates opposing views. Have students write the question on their Discussion Web.

3. Have students work with a partner to brainstorm at least three responses for each side of the question posed. Encourage students to write down key words or phrases and strive to have an equal number of reasons in each column. Students could take turns writing reasons on the same Discussion Web. Provide ample time for each set of partners to share their reasons.

4. Pair one set of partners with another set of partners so they can compare their reasons. Tell the groups that the goal is to work toward consensus. Provide time for students to share and discuss. Encourage students to listen carefully, especially for views that may differ from their own. The conclusion can be written in the box on the bottom of the sheet.

5. Select or have each group select an individual to serve as a group spokesperson. Provide three to five minutes for each group to decide which of the group's reasons best support the group's conclusion and check or star the best reasons. Then have the spokesperson from each group report to the whole class.

6. If desired, invite students to write their individual answers to the question posed on the Discussion Web.

7. Consider the following variations of the Discussion Web based on Alvermann (1991) and Swafford (1990).

   - Current or historical issues can be explored by making simple changes in the Discussion Web. The U.S. Civil War slavery issue could be examined through the positions of Stephen A. Douglas and Abraham Lincoln. A partial Discussion Web showing this example follows.

Focus
Comprehension
Response

Text Type
Narrative
Informational

When to Use
After Reading

Strategy
Inferring
Determining Importance
Synthesizing

How to Use
Small Group
Whole Group

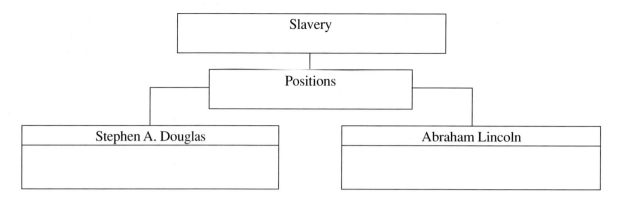

- Before reading a selection, adapt the Discussion Web to stimulate the students' predictions. In the short story titled "Cheating Mr. Diskin," students could complete a Discussion Web adapted as follows.

The story could be read to see which, if any, of the predictions are supported.

- For word problems in mathematics, students can be asked to classify the information from the word problems as relevant or irrelevant in an effort to focus on what is necessary to solve the problem. An example is shown below.

Hem was 12. Scott was 13. Carlos was also 13. The three boys reported their classes' results for the food drive. Hem's class collected 27 items. Scott's class collected 32 items, and Carlos' class collected 39 items. What was the average number of items collected for the food drive?

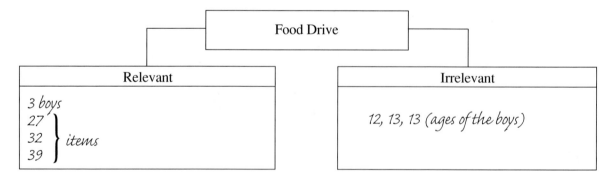

References

Alvermann, D. (1991). The discussion web: A graphic aid for learning across the curriculum. *The Reading Teacher, 45*, 92–99.

Duthie, J. (1986). The web: A powerful tool for the teaching and evaluation of the expository essay. *The History and Social Studies Teacher, 21*, 232–236.

Swafford, J. (1990, July). *Discussion strategies for improving reading and writing to learn.* Paper presented at the World Congress on Reading, Stockholm, Sweden.

Question

Should athletic teams use Indians as mascots?

Reasons

No	Yes
1. Indians are people—not mascots	1. represents school pride
2. represents ethnic insensitivity	2. has been used for many years
3. many major organizations condemn this practice	3. many people favor it

Conclusion

The tradition should be changed to reduce potential conflict.

NAME _____   DATE _____

Discussion Web

Question

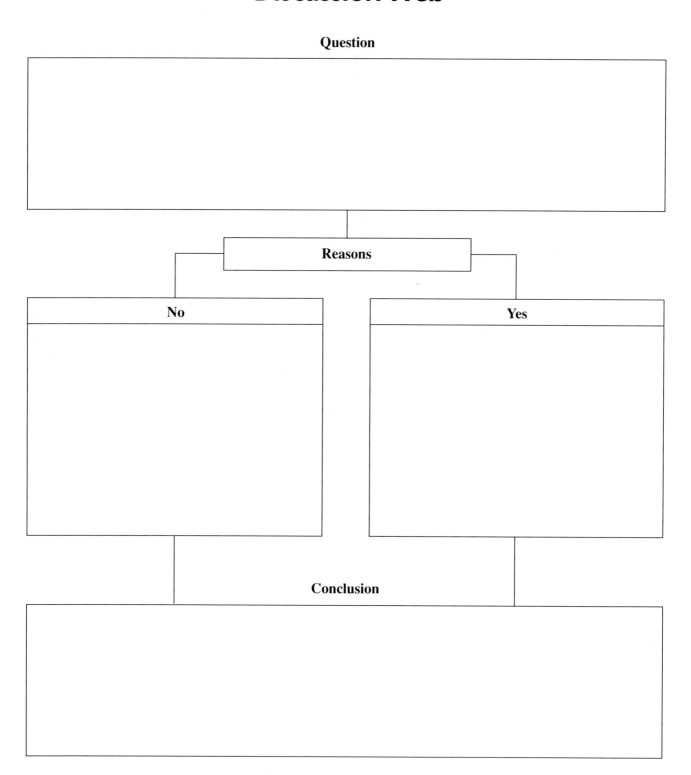

Reasons

No

Yes

Conclusion

Double-Entry Journal

DESCRIPTION: Double-Entry Journals (Tovani, 2000) are a form of guided note taking that help students track their thinking and interact with text while reading. Similar in format to two-column notes, Double-Entry Journals are more flexible and allow students to respond to their reading in a variety of ways. For example, by making connections, noting confusing parts, listing interesting facts or details, drawing a sketch, or noting a difficult vocabulary word, students can respond to their reading and expand their thinking.

Procedure

1. Have students fold a piece of paper in half lengthwise or provide copies of one of the Double-Entry Journal reproducibles on pages 33–34 or on the website.

2. Explain to students that on the left side of the paper, they will copy sentences or words from the text, noting the page(s) where they can be found.

3. On the right side of the paper, students should write their thinking related to the ideas they have written on the left side of the paper. For example, you might say the following.

   Today I am going to read a section of our current events newspaper aloud and show you how I track my thinking as I read by using my Double-Entry Journal. There are several ways that I could respond to the reading, but today I am going to use, "I wonder . . ." to focus my thinking.

4. Read a section of the text aloud. As you read, write down a quotation or word that you have a question about. For example, you might say the following.

   In our text it says that 300 million Africans lack access to safe water. On the left side of my paper I am going to write, "Bad water" and note that it is discussed on page 1.

   On the right side of my paper I am going to write, "I wonder what caused the problem?"

5. Continue modeling your note taking and What I Wonder questions until you think that students understand how to proceed.

6. Invite students to work individually or in pairs to read the remainder of the selection and create notes and questions using their Double-Entry Journals.

7. When students have completed the reading, invite them to read their quotations and questions and use them as a basis for a class discussion of the reading.

8. Tovani (2000) suggests starting with one response prompt and providing practice opportunities for students before introducing additional response options for use in the Double-Entry Journals.

9. Additional reproducibles can be found on the website.

Reference

Tovani, C. (2000). *I read it, but I don't get it: Comprehension strategies for adolescent readers*. Portland, ME: Stenhouse.

Focus
Comprehension
Response

Text Type
Narrative
Informational

When to Use
During Reading

Strategy
Monitoring Meaning
Asking Questions
Inferring
Determining Importance
Synthesizing

How to Use
Individual
Small Group

Double-Entry Journal

Title _Water: Stuff of Life, Death_

What the Text Says	What I Wonder
1. Bad water—300 million Africans lack access to safe water. Page _1_	1. I wonder what caused the problem?
2. Government doesn't work. Page _3_	2. I wonder what the government of Malawi is like? I wonder why they don't do something?
3. The best solutions come from sitting down as close to the problem as possible and talking with the people. Page _4_	3. I wonder if this isn't the best way to solve most problems?
4. Cell phones, e-mail, and migrants are connecting Africa with urban America. Page _5_	4. I wonder how Africans get the cell phones when they can't get to fresh water?
5. Water for People is making a difference. Page _6_	5. I wonder how we could help this cause? I wonder if our Student Council could sponsor this?

Double-Entry Journal

Title _____

What the Text Says	What I Wonder
1. Page _____	1.
2. Page _____	2.
3. Page _____	3.
4. Page _____	4.
5. Page _____	5.
6. Page _____	6.

Double-Entry Journal

Title _____

What the Text Says	What I Think
1. Page _____	1.
2. Page _____	2.
3. Page _____	3.
4. Page _____	4.
5. Page _____	5.
6. Page _____	6.

Exit Slips

DESCRIPTION: Exit Slips (Lenski & Johns, 2004; Short, Harste, & Burke, 1996) are quick ways to invite student response after learning. Exit Slips are completed at the end of a class period and are generally collected by the teacher as students leave the room. Exit Slips provide quick feedback for the teacher about how well students understood the lesson and what might need to be addressed in a future lesson.

Focus
Response

Text Type
Narrative
Informational

When to Use
After Reading

Strategy
Asking Questions
Synthesizing

How to Use
Individual

Procedure

1. Consider the type of response you wish to receive from your students.
2. Reproduce one of the Exit Slips from the reproducible master on page 36 or ask students to respond to one or more of the following queries prior to the end of class:
   - Today I learned . . .
   - I don't understand . . .
   - I would like to learn more about . . .
   - A question I have is . . .
   - Please explain more about . . .
   - The most important thing I learned today is . . .
   - The thing that surprised me most today was . . .
   - I wish . . .
   - The best part of class today was . . .
3. After your lesson, distribute the Exit Slip or direct students to respond to one or more of the stems above. See the example below.
4. As students leave the classroom or at the completion of the lesson, collect the slips. Use student responses to guide follow-up instruction.

References

Lenski, S. D., & Johns, J. L. (2004). *Improving writing: K–8 Strategies, assessments, and resources* (2nd ed.). Dubuque, IA: Kendall Hunt.

Short, K. G., Harste, J. C., & Burke, C. (1996). *Creating classrooms for authors and inquirers* (2nd ed.). Portsmouth, NH: Heinemann.

Sample Exit Slip for Middle School Geography

I would like to learn more about . . . *whether global warming is really a problem and how it might affect me.*

I wish . . . *we could work with our partners more often in class.*

Name _____ Date _____

Exit Slip

3　Things I Learned

_____

_____

_____

2　Things I Found Interesting

_____

_____

1　Question I Still Have

_____

_____

- ✂

Name _____ Date _____

Subject _____ Period _____

Vocabulary Exit Slip

Three words I learned today are:

a) _____ b) _____ c) _____

Here is one of the words in a sentence:

_____

_____

_____

- ✂

Name _____ Date _____

Subject _____ Period _____

Exit Slip

Today I learned that:

_____

_____

It is important because:

_____

_____

Four Square

DESCRIPTION: Four Square (Lenski, Wham, Johns, & Caskey, 2011) is an easy-to-use strategy that helps students learn meanings for new words. Because students are asked to make personal associations with the new word, word learning and retention may be enhanced.

Procedure

1. Draw a square with four quadrants on the board. Label them as shown in the example below.

Word	Personal Clue or Connection
Definition	**Opposite**

2. Tell students that you are sharing a strategy that will help them learn and remember important vocabulary words. Then write a vocabulary word in the upper-left quadrant. Invite a student to pronounce the word.

3. Ask students to offer words, phrases, or experiences that they personally associate with the vocabulary word. Write one of their associations in the upper-right quadrant. An alternative for words may be a picture or logo that is drawn in one of the quadrants.

4. Invite a student who may know the meaning of the word to offer it. Encourage other students to react to the definition and provide clarification as needed. Then write a brief, student-friendly definition of the word in the lower-left quadrant.

5. Have students offer words or phrases that are opposite in meaning. Discuss the responses and select a word or phrase to write in the lower-right quadrant.

6. Give students copies made from the Four Square reproducible master on page 39. Provide words from a reading selection for students to use. Have students work individually to complete their squares. Then provide time for students to discuss their squares in groups of three to five students.

7. Clarify the meanings of the words selected with the whole group.

8. Have students use the Four Square strategy independently with words you believe to be important in understanding the content of your lesson or unit of study.

Reference

Lenski, S. D., Wham, M. A., Johns, J. L., & Caskey, M. M. (2011). *Reading and learning strategies: Middle grades through high school* (4th ed.). Dubuque, IA: Kendall Hunt.

Focus
Vocabulary

Text Type
Narrative
Informational

When to Use
Before Reading
After Reading

Strategy
Using Prior Knowledge
Synthesizing

How to Use
Individual
Small Group
Whole Group

Sample of Four Square for *Science*

Word	Personal Clue or Connection
electrolysis	chlorine is made from electrolysis and put in our drinking water

Definition	Opposite
electrical energy is used to bring about a change	corrosion—solutions transfer electrons and break down metals

Sample of Four Square for *Social Studies*

Word	Personal Clue or Connection
stifle	to dampen the spirit

Definition	Opposite
to smother to prevent	enable

Four Square

Word	Personal Clue or Connection
Definition	**Opposite**

Word	Personal Clue or Connection
Definition	**Opposite**

Frayer Model

DESCRIPTION: The Frayer Model (Frayer, Fredrick, & Klausmeier, 1969) is a categorization activity that helps students develop a thorough understanding of important concepts. It also provides a visual means of distinguishing items that help define the concept from those that are merely associated with it.

Procedure

1. Display the reproducible master on page 43.

2. Select a key word or concept from the lesson, for example, *ecosystem*.

3. Generate a list of key characteristics of the concept. Key characteristics for *ecosystem* might be *relationships, interactions, surroundings, living things*, and *nonliving things*.

4. Introduce the concept to students and show them your list of the key characteristics. Using the reproducible master on page 43, make copies for the students. In small cooperative groups, have students generate examples of the concept. Record responses on the Frayer Model graphic organizer. Examples of ecosystems might be *forests, cities, deserts*, and *oceans*.

5. Have students read the selection and check to see if the characteristics and examples are accurate. Take time to clarify meaning for nonessential characteristics and nonexamples.

6. Have students add nonessential characteristics and nonexamples of the concept to their organizer. Some items from their original list of characteristics and examples may need to be moved to other sections of the model based on their reading and collaborating with their peers. Depending on the specific ecosystem under consideration, nonessential characteristics of an ecosystem might be *glaciers, insects, buildings*, or *birds*. Nonexamples of an ecosystem might be *automobiles, solutions*, or *electricity*.

7. Once students are secure in the essential and nonessential characteristics as well as examples and nonexamples of the concept, have them relate the concept to a subordinate concept, a superordinate concept, and, finally, a coordinate term. For example, a subordinate concept for ecosystem might be *habitat*. A superordinate concept might be *environment*. A similar or coordinate phrase might be *community of organisms*.

8. An additional reproducible and sample can be found on the website.

Reference

Frayer, D. A., Fredrick, W. C., & Klausmeier, H. J. (1969). *A schema for testing the level of concept mastery: Report from the project on situational variables and efficiency of concept learning.* Madison, WI: Wisconsin Research and Development Center for Cognitive Learning.

Focus
Vocabulary

Text Type
Narrative
Informational

When to Use
Before Reading
After Reading

Strategy
Determining Importance
Synthesizing

How to Use
Small Group
Whole Group

Sample Frayer Model for **Biology**

Essential Characteristics	Nonessential Characteristics
Have organized nuclei Flagella or cilia Unicellular Microscopic Live in water or damp places	Contain chlorophyll Sexual Asexual Capture food

PROTIST

Examples	Nonexamples
Euglena Diatoms Protozoa Slime molds Paramecia	Animals Fungi Plants Monerans

A word that means about the same as protist is _____ protista _____.

A word that is more general than protist is _____ organism _____.

A word that is more specific than protist is _____ protozoa _____.

Sample Frayer Model for **Math**

Essential Characteristics	Nonessential Characteristics
Natural elements, their opposites, and zero Is a number Has no fraction part Has no decimal part	The "+" sign May be positive May be negative May be zero

INTEGER

Examples	Nonexamples
5 100 −73 2 0 325	$\frac{-15}{2}$ 1.25 0.5 $\sqrt{2}$

A word that means about the same as integer is _____ signed number _____.

A word that is more general than integer is _____ rational number _____.

A word that is more specific than integer is _____ whole number _____.

Frayer Model

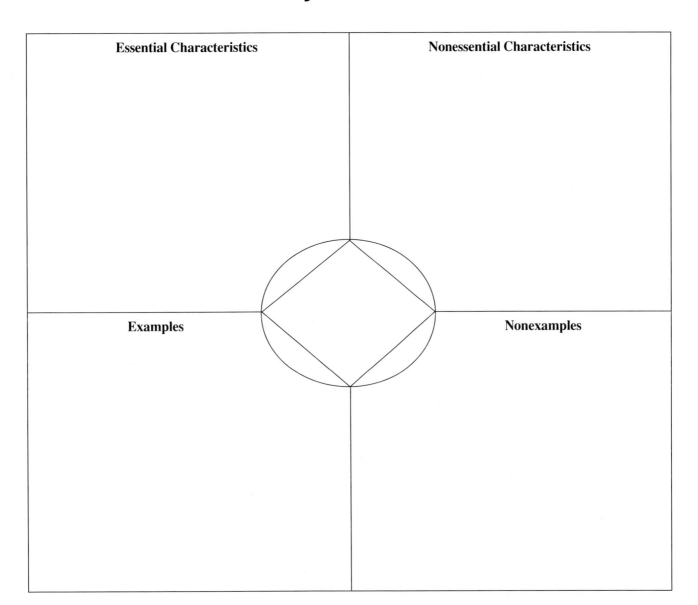

A word that means about the same as the key term is _____.

A word that is more general than the key term is _____.

A word that is more specific than the key term is _____.

Info Boxes

Focus
Vocabulary
Comprehension

Text Type
Narrative
Informational

When to Use
After Reading

Strategy
Inferring
Determining Importance
Synthesizing

How to Use
Individual
Small Group
Whole Group

DESCRIPTION: Info Boxes (adapted from Allen, 2000; Beers, 2003; and Hoyt, 2008) provide a way for students to recall and organize information about a chapter or topic after reading or learning about it. The completed grid can be used to stimulate discussion, determine main ideas and details, and create summaries. Completed grids can also be used as information sources for more extended writing projects.

Procedure

1. Create a grid containing one or more letters of the alphabet in each box of the grid or use one of the graphic organizers on pages 47–48 or from the website.

2. Write the title at the top of the grid and duplicate copies for students.

3. At the completion of a chapter or unit of study, distribute copies of the grid to students. You might say the following.

   We have been studying pond scum. Think about the information we have gained through our text reading, our Internet research, our laboratory work, and our visit to Coal Creek. Work with your laboratory partner and try to record one or more ideas in each box of the grid. Each of the ideas in the grid must start with the letter or one of the letters of the alphabet that are written in the grid.

4. When students have completed the task, say the following.

   Look at the grid of information you have developed. Review the information with your partner. Decide which ideas in the grid are the most important and circle them.

5. When students have determined the most important information, encourage them to write a summary and share it orally with the class.

6. Students may also use the ideas in the grid as a basis for developing a longer piece of writing on the topic.

7. Info Boxes are also excellent resources for use in review and test preparation.

References

Allen, J. (2000). *Yellow brick roads: Shared and guided paths to independent reading 4–12.* Portland, ME: Stenhouse.

Beers, K. (2003). *When kids can't read, what teachers can do.* Portsmouth, NH: Heinemann.

Hoyt, L. (2008). *Revisit, reflect, retell: Time-tested strategies for teaching reading comprehension.* Portsmouth, NH: Heinemann.

Sample Info Boxes for **Biology**

Title _____ The Promise of Pond Scum _____

A Alga can produce hydrogen After photosynthesis process	**B**	**C** Convert solar energy directly into hydrogen (electricity) Coal alternative	**D** Depleted fossil fuels
E Enzymes	**F** Fuel consumption growing	**G** Golden, Colorado Green algae Gluttonous demand for power Gas alternative	**H** Hydrogenase enzymes
I	**J**	**K**	**L** Living organisms
M Manipulate photosynthesis Microbes	**N** National Renewable Energy Lab	**O**	**P** Photosynthesis-to-hydrogen process Photovoltaics expensive and inefficient Photosynthesis original source of fossil fuels
Q	**R** Resources depleted	**S** Sunlight needed for photosynthesis	**T** Turn solar rays into molecular energy Twenty million barrels of oil a day
U	**V**	**W** Withhold sulfate	**XYZ**

Info Boxes

Title _____

A	B	C	D
E	F	G	H
I	J	K	L
M	N	O	P
Q	R	S	T
U	V	W	XYZ

Info Boxes

Title _____

AB	**CD**	**EF**	**GH**
IJ	**KL**	**MN**	**OP**
QRS	**TU**	**VW**	**XYZ**

Summary: _____

_____

_____

_____

_____

_____

_____

Informational Text Structures

Focus
Comprehension

Text Type
Informational

When to Use
During Reading
After Reading

Strategy
Using Prior Knowledge
Asking Questions
Inferring
Determining Importance
Synthesizing

How to Use
Individual
Small Group
Whole Group

DESCRIPTION: The use of graphic organizers to help teach the five major types of Informational Text Structures can be a powerful way to help students organize and represent ideas. Graphic organizers can also serve as a framework for recording notes for review and study. Graphic organizers may be considered similar to outlining but with much more flexibility.

Procedure

1. A succinct overview of the five major types of Informational Text Structures found in content area materials can be found on page 51. Review the five text structures and select one to present to your students that is represented in your instructional materials. Examples for the five text structures in history are found on page 52.

2. Tell students that you will be modeling the use of graphic organizers to help them understand how the information in a text is organized so they can better understand and remember the material.

3. Show the graphic organizer and model how to complete it. For example, you might say something like the following if the compare/contrast example on page 58 is used.

   Look at the brief passage about the English language that I've given you and follow along as I read it. [Read the passage.] Look at the text pattern I'm showing you. You can see that it is comparison and contrast. There is no title so I won't fill that in, but who or what is being compared? [Invite a student to respond.] That's right; it's comparing two versions of the English language. I'll write that phrase here on the organizer. Now let's see if we can list some ways the two variations of English are alike and different. [Guide students as needed and complete the organizer.]

4. Duplicate the reproducible on page 58 and distribute copies to students. Then use an example from your content area that is the same type of text structure that you modeled. Have students read the appropriate text selection and complete the organizer. You may initially want students to work with a partner or in small groups.

5. Give students time to complete the organizer and then have whole class sharing. Clarify and expand student responses as needed.

6. Systematically introduce other graphic organizers using a similar procedure as opportunities arise. Be sure to help students understand how graphic organizers can be used for clarification of concepts, review, and study. See pages 53–61 for reproducibles to use with different text structures.

7. As students become more familiar with graphic organizers, you may want to introduce the signal words listed on page 50 that are often associated with particular organizers. They can be helpful cues to students as they read to help them identify particular text structures.

8. Once the text structures appropriate for your content area have been taught, you may want to enlarge or adapt page 51 as a concise summary that can be part of a bulletin board or a review sheet given to students for reference and use.

Main Idea/Details (Description)

For instance	Also	In addition to	Specifically
For example	Such as	In other words	Furthermore
To begin with	In fact	As	Most important
That is	Along with		

Time Order/Sequence

First	At	Next	When
Second	Not long after	Then	Before
Third	Now	Last	Earlier
On (date)	During	Later	

Compare/Contrast

However	Like/unlike	Although	Rather
On the other hand	In contrast	Instead	Most
But	On the contrary	Otherwise	Same
Yet	Likewise	While	As opposed to
As well as	Similarly		

Cause/Effect

Because	Consequently	Subsequently	Due to
If/then	As a result	So	This led to
Since	Nevertheless	For this reason	So that
Therefore	Thus		

Problem/Solution

Problem is	If/then	Question/answer	A solution is
Question is	Because	Conclude	Propose that
Dilemma is	So that		

Informational Text Structures

Text Pattern	Description	Signal Words	Graphic Organizer
Main Idea/Details (Description)	Key concept or idea and details about characteristics, attributes, features, actions, examples	For instance, for example, to begin with, that is, also, such as, in fact, along with, in addition to, in other words, as, specifically, furthermore, most important	
Time Order/Sequence	Information is given in chronological or numerical order	First, second, third, on (date), at, not long after, now, during, next, then, last, later, when, before, earlier	
Compare/Contrast	How two or more things are alike and/or different	However, on the other hand, but, yet, as well as, like/unlike, in contrast, similarly, on the contrary, likewise, although, instead, otherwise, while, rather, most, same, as opposed to	
Cause/Effect	Ideas, events, or facts are presented with effects or facts that happen as a result	Because, if/then, since, therefore, consequently, as a result, nevertheless, thus, subsequently, so, for this reason, due to, this led to, so that	
Problem/Solution	A problem is stated with one or more solutions offered	Problem is, question is, dilemma is, if/then, because, so that, question/answer, conclude, a solution is, propose that	

Text Structures and Examples

Main Idea/Supporting Details (Description)

A key concept or idea is presented followed by more information about the concept or idea.

Example

Main Idea   The monarchs themselves were regularly in France.

Details   William I spent half his reign in Normandy. William II and Henry I also spent half of their reigns there, as did Henry II, who lived there for as many as twenty years.

Time Order/Sequence

Information is given in the order that it happened or in a sequence.

Example

By the thirteenth century, English was the dominant language in the Lowland south and east. By 1400 the Scottish dialect had evolved. By the 1500s, it was clear that a standard dialect was emerging throughout the land.

Compare/Contrast

Information shows how two or more things are alike and/or different.

Example

Two variations of the English language emerged, Middle English and Standard English. Both were used throughout the land, but different regions began to use one or the other predominantly.

In Middle English, all dialects were equal and written language contained a wide range of forms, each being acceptable. No one minded if a writer spelled a word differently in different parts of the same text.

With the rise of Standard English, agreement arose about how things should be said and written. As more people became able to read and write, the need for norms grew. There was a growing sense of shared usage.

Cause/Effect

Ideas, events, or facts are presented with things that happen as a result.

Example

As more people became able to read and write, the need for a standardized language became apparent.

Problem/Solution

A problem is given and one or more solutions are offered.

Example

In the 1500s, there was a huge amount of variation in how language was used and written. As more people learned to read and write, the variation in language usage hindered communication. In order to solve the problem, people needed to work together to develop a common style. Many people needed to interact regularly and frequently.

Main Idea and Supporting Details Text Pattern

Supporting Detail

Supporting Detail

Main Idea

Supporting Detail

Supporting Detail

Main Idea and Supporting Details Text Pattern

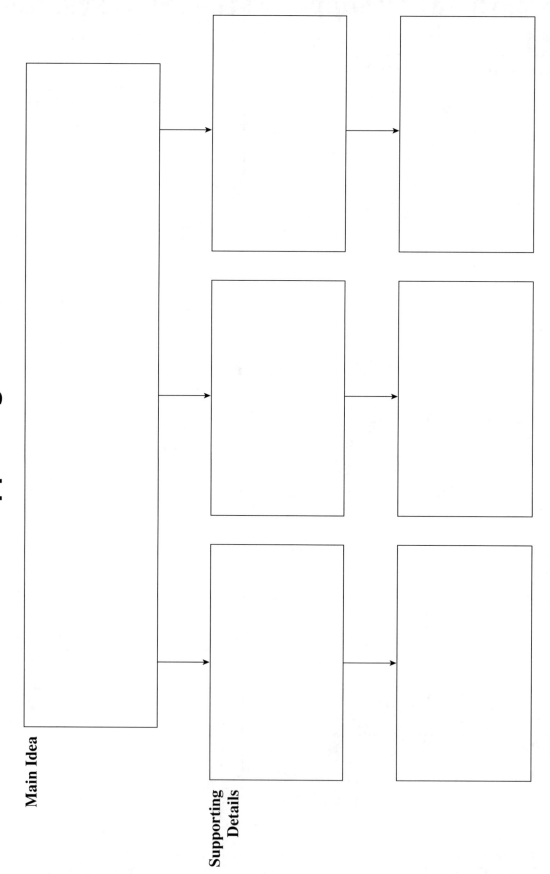

Main Idea

Supporting Details

Main Idea and Supporting Details Text Pattern

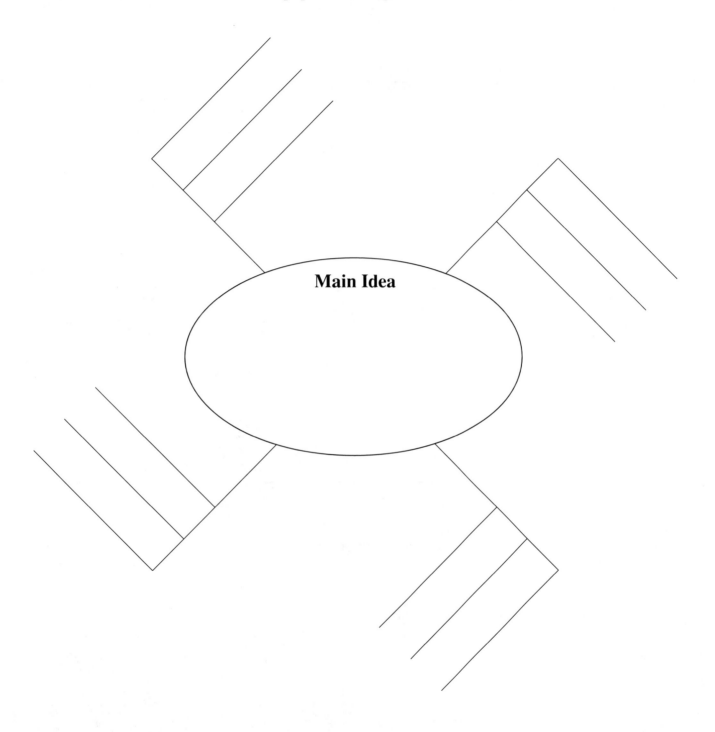

Main Idea

Sequence of Events Text Pattern

Compare and Contrast Text Pattern

Compare and Contrast Text Pattern

```
┌─────────────────────────────────────────────────────────┐
│ Title                                                     │
│                                                           │
│                                                           │
│                                                           │
└─────────────────────────────────────────────────────────┘
                              │
                              ▼
┌─────────────────────────────────────────────────────────┐
│ Who or what is being compared?                            │
│                                                           │
│                                                           │
│                                                           │
└─────────────────────────────────────────────────────────┘
        │                                       │
        ▼                                       ▼
┌──────────────────────┐          ┌──────────────────────┐
│ How are they alike?   │          │ How are they different? │
│                       │          │                       │
│                       │          │                       │
│                       │          │                       │
│                       │          │                       │
│                       │          │                       │
│                       │          │                       │
│                       │          │                       │
└──────────────────────┘          └──────────────────────┘
```

Cause and Effect Text Pattern

CAUSE

[ ]

EFFECT

[ ]

Why Something Happens

[ ]

What Happens

[ ]

[ ] → [ ]

[ ] → [ ]

[ ] → [ ]

[ ] → [ ]

[ ] → [ ]

[ ] → [ ]

Cause and Effect Text Pattern:
Chain of Related Events

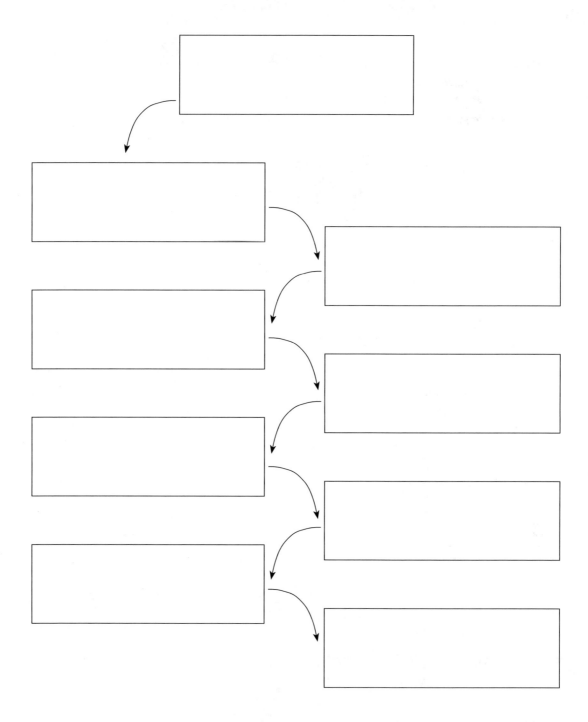

Problem and Solution Text Pattern

Problem

Attempts

Outcomes

Solution

Intra-Act

DESCRIPTION: The Intra-Act strategy (Hoffman, 1979) encourages students to construct their own decisions about issues by making intertextual links. In four steps, students move from formulating opinions based solely upon one text to ultimately basing their opinions upon further research, group discussions, and reflection. The four steps are: 1) students construct meaning from a text selection; 2) students make connections between the information in the first text and other resources they find on the topic; 3) students share their own feelings on the topic and the values those feelings convey; and 4) students reflect on the newly formed values.

Procedure

1. Duplicate copies of the Intra-Act reproducible master on page 65 or adapt it to suit your needs or purposes.

2. Explain to students the difference between topics that are explanatory, such as how a bill becomes a law, and topics that are subject to opinion, such as whether certain bills should become laws.

3. Use the sample topic and chart on page 64 or develop an example from your curriculum to demonstrate to students how the Intra-Act strategy works. Show examples of statements to the students. Brainstorm with students other statements that could be made to stimulate debate and discussion on the sample topic.

4. Either on your own or with students' input, choose another controversial topic for which you can find several sources. The topic should be one that readily lends itself to differing opinions.

5. Assign the first reading on the controversial topic. Following the reading, brainstorm with students possible opinion statements that can be made about the reading. It should be possible to answer the statements with either yes or no. Choose four of the statements and write them under *Statements* on the reproducible master. Duplicate copies of the reproducible master for students.

6. Assign students to work in small heterogeneous groups (3 to 4 students per group). The groups should take seven to ten minutes to summarize and discuss the reading. Assign a leader in each group to write or report the summary of the reading.

7. Allow students class time to research their topics using other literature and media. You may wish to enlist the help of your school's librarian or media specialist to provide a wide variety of relevant material for your classroom. Instruct students to be prepared to share and discuss their findings in their next group meeting.

8. Schedule time for students to meet in their small groups to compare their research findings and any conclusions they have drawn about the topic.

9. After students have explored the topic more thoroughly, they will begin the valuative phase of the discussion. In this phase, students work independently. First, students fill in the names of each of their group members across the top row of the grid. Next, they write yes or no under their own name in response

Focus
Comprehension

Text Type
Narrative
Informational

When to Use
After Reading

Strategy
Using Prior Knowledge
Asking Questions
Inferring
Synthesizing

How to Use
Individual
Small Group
Whole Group

63

to each statement. Finally, they predict how each member of their group will respond to the statements and write yes or no under each member's names after each statement.

10. Students meet again with their groups and share their responses to the statements. As each student shares, the other group members compare the student's responses to their predictions.

11. Finally, open the discussion to the whole class. Encourage students to share the reasons for their responses, and allow opportunities to challenge, support, and question one another. This is an opportune time to reinforce student skills of offering constructive criticism and disagreeing respectfully and assertively, not aggressively.

Reference

Hoffman, J. V. (1979). The intra-act procedure for critical reading. *Journal of Reading, 22*, 605–608.

Sample of Intra-Act for **Social Studies**

Topic _____ Was it appropriate for the United States to enter into the Iraq War? _____

(Write group members' names, including your own, in the top row of blanks.)

Statements	José	Anna	Tom	Xiao Peng
The U.S. has an obligation to enforce justice and world peace.				
We had no business being across the world in someone else's fight.				
We (the U.S.) were the best candidates to eliminate Saddam Hussein.				
We should have spent all the money that was spent on the Iraq War on our public schools instead.				

Intra-Act

Topic _____

(Write group members' names, including your own, in the top row of blanks.)

Statements				

Directions

1. Think about the above statements and then under your name write *yes* if you agree with the statement or *no* if you disagree with the statement.

2. Under each member's name, predict how that person will respond to the statements by writing *yes* or *no* by each statement under the name.

3. When you meet with your group, compare your predictions to how members really answered.

4. When the class meets to discuss the statements, use the information you found in your research to help you challenge, support, or question your own and others' opinions. Remember to listen well, support your responses with your research, and be respectful to others in your responses.

Knowledge Rating

DESCRIPTION: Knowledge Rating (Blachowicz, 1986; Blachowicz & Fisher, 2009) is a prereading activity that encourages students to develop sensitivity to and awareness of words by responding to a list of words that reflects the content of the lesson. This self-evaluation strategy serves to activate prior knowledge and helps students to make predictions about what is to be learned. Using the Knowledge Rating sheet and participating in related discussion helps students understand that word meanings evolve with use and experience. A deepening understanding of words evolves over time with high-quality instruction.

Procedure

1. Select several vocabulary words that reflect the content of the lesson.

2. Write these words on the Knowledge Rating reproducible master on page 69 or on one of the reproducibles from the website. Duplicate and distribute it to students or have students copy the words from the overhead projector or board.

3. Invite students to rate their knowledge of each word according to one of the following categories: 1) Know It Well, 2) Think I Know It, 3) Have Heard/ Seen It, and 4) No Clue.

4. Divide your class into small heterogeneous groups and invite students to discuss their knowledge of each word. Invite students to define those words that fall into the *Know It Well* category.

5. Circulate through the classroom while students are discussing the words. Listen to students' comments to determine their knowledge about the subject.

6. Have the small heterogeneous groups return to a whole group setting. Conduct a brief discussion of the words, focusing on particular meanings or features that are appropriate. Invite the students to make predictions about the content of the lesson, based on their expanding knowledge of some of the words contained in it. For example, you might say, "Looking at these words, what do you think we might find out about in this lesson?"

7. Record students' ideas on the board.

8. As students participate in the lesson, be aware of the words as they are encountered, and determine if their predictions were correct. If the words are from a reading selection, encourage students to use the context when it will help clarify word meanings.

References

Blachowicz, C. L. Z. (1986). Making connections: Alternatives to the vocabulary notebook. *Journal of Reading, 29,* 643–649.

Blachowicz, C., & Fisher, P. (2009). *Teaching vocabulary in all classrooms* (4th ed.). Upper Saddle River, NJ: Pearson.

Focus
Vocabulary

Text Type
Narrative
Informational

When to Use
Before Reading
After Reading

Strategy
Using Prior Knowledge

How to Use
Individual
Small Group
Whole Group

Sample Knowledge Rating for High School *Math*

Directions: Below are some words that you will find in your lesson. Rate your knowledge for each of the words by placing a ✓ under the category you have chosen.

Word	(1) Know It Well	(2) Think I Know It	(3) Have Heard/Seen It	(4) No Clue
intercepts		✓		
x-axis			✓	
zero	✓			
vertex				✓
symmetry				✓
maximum	✓			
minimum	✓			

Knowledge Rating

Directions: Below are some words that you will find in your lesson. Rate your knowledge for each of the words by placing an X under the category you have chosen.

Word	(1) Know It Well	(2) Think I Know It	(3) Have Heard/Seen It	(4) No Clue

Know-Want-Learned Plus (K-W-L Plus)

DESCRIPTION: The K-W-L Plus strategy stimulates students' background knowledge before learning and organizes their knowledge after learning. The K-W-L strategy was originally developed as **K**—What I Know, **W**—What I Want to Find Out, **L**—What I Learned and Still Need to Learn (Ogle, 1986). The addition of Plus (Carr & Ogle, 1987) adds a writing opportunity for students to summarize their knowledge, add their personal response, and/or organize their learning through the use of a Concept Map or Semantic Map (see reproducible masters on pages 25 and 78).

The K-W-L Plus strategy is easy to use and helps students access their knowledge about a topic prior to reading or learning more about it. By developing a list of questions of what students want or expect to learn, they establish purposes for reading and/or learning. The strategy invites students to clarify their preconceptions about the topic by cross-checking after the reading or learning experience. This strategy provides opportunities for misconceptions to be clarified and also may establish the need to obtain additional information in order to answer questions that may not have been addressed in the lesson. The final aspect of the strategy involves having students create a map of information, write a summary of the information learned, and/or write their reactions to the information acquired.

Procedure

1. Display the reproducible master on page 73.

2. Select a topic and invite students to think about what they already know about it. Remind them that making connections now will help them better understand the lesson.

3. Write students' ideas under the **K** heading.

4. Ask students what they want to know or expect to learn about the topic. Record their questions under the **W** heading. You may wish to guide students in thinking about questions that lead toward major concepts in the lesson or unit.

5. Have students read the selection, watch the video, listen to the audiotape, or participate in the experiment or field trip, depending on the situation.

6. After the learning experience, have students recall information that they learned. Record their responses under the **L** heading. You may also list ideas that they still need to learn here or create another column labeled S (still need to learn).

7. Help students discern or identify broad categories for the ideas under the **L** heading. A sample completed K-W-L Plus is found on page 72.

8. Create a Semantic Map (see page 78) with the topic in the center and the categories of information around it. Ask students to assist in listing each idea from the L section under the appropriate category.

Focus
Comprehension
Response

Text Type
Narrative
Informational

When to Use
Before Reading
After Reading

Strategy
Using Prior Knowledge
Asking Questions
Inferring
Determining Importance
Synthesizing

How to Use
Individual
Small Group
Whole Group

9. Using the Semantic Map as a guide, have students work individually or in pairs to create a summary paragraph for each category.

10. As students become proficient with the strategy, provide copies of the K-W-L Plus reproducible master on page 73 to students. Encourage students to use K-W-L Plus in future lessons. Additional reproducible masters with variations of this strategy are found on the website.

References

Carr, E., & Ogle, D. (1987). K-W-L Plus: A strategy for comprehension and summarization. *Journal of Reading, 30,* 626–631.

Ogle, D. M. (1986). K-W-L: A teaching model that develops active reading of expository text. *The Reading Teacher, 39,* 564–570.

Sample K-W-L Plus for Intermediate Grade Science

Insect-Eating Plants

K What We Know	W What We Want to Find Out	L What We Learned
Venus flytrap	Why do they eat insects?	N–Plants get nitrogen from insects and spiders.
eat hamburger	How do they get insects to stay?	L–Plants live in swampy areas.
leaves open and close	Are there many plants that eat insects?	P–Plants set traps and wait for insects to come by.
live in wet places	Where are they found?	L–Pitcher plants live in many parts of the United States.
small		P–Digestive fluid dissolves the insects.
eat insects		K–Pitcher plants
		K–Venus flytrap

C Categories of Information
L = Location
K = Kinds
P = Process of Eating
N = Need/Uses of Insects

Summary: *Pitcher plants and Venus flytraps, two kinds of meat-eating plants, live in swampy areas and get needed nutrients by catching and digesting insects and spiders.*

K-W-L Plus Strategy Sheet

Directions: Write the topic of the lesson on the line below. Before the lesson, list what you know under the **K** column. Then think about what you want to know or what you expect you will learn. List these ideas under the **W** column. After the lesson, list what you learned under the **L** column. Then think of categories for the information you learned. List these under the **C** section.

_____

K What We Know	W What We Want to Find Out	L What We Learned

C
Categories of Information

Summary

List-Group-Label (Semantic Mapping)

Focus
Vocabulary
Comprehension

Text Type
Narrative
Informational

When to Use
Before Reading
After Reading

Strategy
Determining Importance
Synthesizing

How to Use
Individual
Small Group
Whole Group

DESCRIPTION: List-Group-Label, also known as Semantic Mapping, when graphically represented (Heimlich & Pittelman, 1986; Johnson & Pearson, 1984; Pearson & Johnson, 1978; Taba, 1967), helps students to organize information in categorical form. By classifying and categorizing information, students become active readers and, in the process, remember new vocabulary and information.

Procedure

1. Choose a major concept or topic being studied by the class. In high school health class, for example, the topic of drug use is a key area.

2. List words related to the topic on the board. Ask students to brainstorm words related to the topic. For example, words related to drug use might be *medicine, illness, substance abuse, illegal drugs, synthetic drugs, gateway drugs, overdose, withdrawal, side effects, addiction, dependence,* and *tolerance.* Try to keep the number of responses to twenty or twenty-five for ease of management.

3. When the brainstormed words have been listed, read them aloud and ask students to cluster the words into smaller groups based on shared relationships. This can be done in list form (List-Group-Label reproducible on page 77) or in graphic form (Semantic Map reproducible on page 78). Students need to label clusters or give them titles to indicate what the words have in common. You may wish to have students complete this step in small cooperative groups. It is often possible for some of the brainstormed words to become category headings. For example, the labels for clusters related to drug use might be: *Helpful Uses of Drugs, Harmful Uses of Drugs,* and *Dangers of Substance Abuse.*

4. When students have completed their classification and categorization of the words, invite students to share the labels for each of their clusters and the words they have included under each heading. You may wish to record these on the board.

5. It is important that students share their reasons for their clustering decisions. This sharing stimulates students to think of the words in a variety of ways, consider their meanings, connect them, and see relationships between and among the words. A List-Group-Label sample is found on page 76.

6. If used as a prereading activity, ask students to read the text and evaluate their classifications. They may need to rearrange some words based on additional information in the lesson.

7. If used as a postreading activity, students may want to return to the text and confirm their reasons for and accuracy of their clusters. Students may also wish to use their completed lists or semantic maps as a study aid.

8. The strategy work can be extended over the course of several days as students acquire additional information about the topic. More words can be added to the clusters as students expand their knowledge and increase the connections they make between and among the words. If desired, different colored inks

can be used for words added from additional sources or at different times, thus graphically illustrating the expanding knowledge base for the students and the desirability of using a variety of resources in acquiring information.

9. When the lists or semantic maps are complete, have students work individually or in pairs to write a summary of the information in one of the clusters or write a longer piece about the topic, using each one of the clusters of information as a paragraph in the longer piece.

References

Heimlich, J. E., & Pittelman, S. D. (1986). *Semantic mapping: Classroom applications.* Newark, DE: International Reading Association.

Johnson, D. D., & Pearson, P. D. (1984). *Teaching reading vocabulary* (2nd ed.). New York: Holt, Rinehart & Winston.

Pearson, P. D., & Johnson, D. D. (1978). *Teaching reading comprehension.* New York: Holt, Rinehart & Winston.

Taba, H. (1967). *Teacher's handbook for elementary social studies.* Reading, MA: Addison-Wesley.

Sample List-Group-Label Developed from a High School Health Lesson on the *Nervous System*

Nervous System
(topic)

1. Brainstorm a list of words related to the topic given to you by your teacher. Write the topic on the line above and list the words that are related to it in the space below.

brain	brain stem	autonomic
somatic	sympathetic	reflexes
cerebellum	spinal cord	parasympathetic
cerebrum	meninges	nerves

2. Now consider how some of the words listed above might be related. Think of ways they might be grouped together by their meanings. Write the title of the categories or headings on each line below. (You may have a greater or lesser number of words and groupings than the number of lines below.) Then list the words under the appropriate headings. Use the back of this paper for additional words and clusters if you need it.

Central Nervous System	Peripheral Nervous System
(cluster heading)	(cluster heading)
1. brain	1. autonomic
2. spinal cord	2. somatic
3. cerebellum	3. sympathetic
4. cerebrum	4. parasympathetic
5. brain stem	5. reflexes
6. meninges	6. nerves

List-Group-Label

_____
(topic)

1. Brainstorm a list of words related to the topic given to you by your teacher. Write the topic on the line above and list the words that are related to it in the space below.

2. Now consider how some of the words listed above might be related. Think of ways they might be grouped together by their meanings. Write the title of the categories or headings on each line below. (You may have a greater or lesser number of words and groupings than the number of lines below.) Then list the words under the appropriate headings. Use the back of this paper for additional words and clusters if you need it.

_____   _____
(cluster heading)   (cluster heading)

1. _____   1. _____
2. _____   2. _____
3. _____   3. _____
4. _____   4. _____
5. _____   5. _____

_____   _____
(cluster heading)   (cluster heading)

1. _____   1. _____
2. _____   2. _____
3. _____   3. _____
4. _____   4. _____
5. _____   5. _____

Semantic Map

_____
(topic)

Directions: Think of ways the ideas from your lesson might be clustered together. Below is one way you might begin to cluster them into categories. You may add to the map below or create a map of your own on the back of this page.

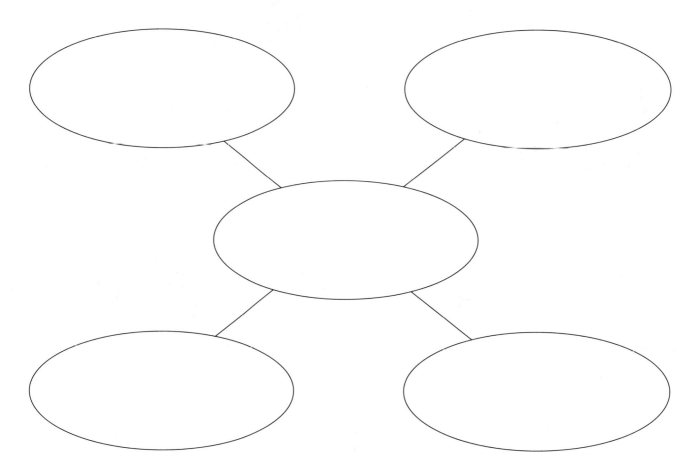

Summary:

People Search

DESCRIPTION: People Search (Hemmrich, Lim, & Neel, 1994) invites students to ask other students in the class for information about a topic or area of study. As students seek specific information, they can become more motivated to learn about a topic and may become more engaged in learning. People Search can be used as a way to introduce a new topic or as a review for a unit of study that has been completed.

Procedure

1. Decide which variation of People Search to use: an introduction to a new course or unit of study, a chapter from a text, or as a review technique for concepts, ideas, and details that were taught.

2. Prepare a list of statements relating to the topic or area of study using the People Search reproducible on page 81. For example, if students are going to read *To Kill a Mockingbird*, you might use statements like the following.

   Find someone who has attended a court trial.

   Find someone who has lived in the South.

3. Duplicate the statements in the People Search and give a copy to each student. Explain that they are to circulate in the room and locate classmates who fit the statement or can answer the question. When a classmate is found, he or she should initial or sign on the line beside the item.

   Find someone who has attended a court trial. _Rosie_____

   Find someone who has lived in the South. _Chad_____

4. Specify if you want students to have as many different signatures as possible or if there is a limit to the number of times an individual student can sign or initial statements.

5. Provide time for students to circulate among classmates in order to complete the People Search. Expect some noise and spirited interactions. Tell students when they have two minutes left for their search.

6. Have students return to their seats. Engage them in a discussion of their search. The discussion can be in small groups or with the entire class. Invite students who signed statements to share with the entire class. For example, if Rosie attended a court trial, have her share a bit about the experience. If both Patrice and Chad lived in the South, have them share where they lived and what it was like. They could also compare it to where they now live.

Reference

Hemmrich, H., Lim, W., & Neel, K. (1994). *Primetime!* Portsmouth, NH: Heinemann.

Focus
Vocabulary
Comprehension
Response

Text Type
Narrative
Informational

When to Use
Before Reading
After Reading

Strategy
Using Prior Knowledge
Inferring

How to Use
Whole Group

Sample People Search for *Literature*

Directions: Before we begin reading *To Kill a Mockingbird*, find other students who can relate to the sentences. Have the student sign his or her name. No student can be listed more than twice. You have seven minutes to try to complete your search.

1. Find someone who vividly remembers his or her first day of school.   _Aliya_

2. Find someone who has been scared of a neighbor in the past.   _Pedro_

3. Find someone who secretly gave a nice gift to someone else.   _Melanie_

4. Find someone who has had a fire in his or her home.   _Martin_

5. Find someone who has attended a court trial.   _Jayden_

6. Find someone who has a friend he or she sees every summer, only in the summer.   _Victoria_

7. Find someone who knows someone who has run away.   _Amarrionn_

8. Find someone who has experienced prejudice.   _Ivanay_

9. Find someone who has lived in the South.   _Ruthamar_

People Search

Directions: Find other students who "fit" the statement or can answer the question. The same student can sign two of the items.

Statement/Questions	**Student**

1. _____ _____

_____

2. _____ _____

_____

3. _____ _____

_____

4. _____ _____

_____

5. _____ _____

_____

6. _____ _____

_____

7. _____ _____

_____

8. _____ _____

_____

9. _____ _____

_____

10. _____ _____

_____

Plot/Concept Relationships

DESCRIPTION: Originally called the Plot Relationships chart (Schmidt & Buckley, 1991), this strategy can be used with narrative text to teach story grammar and with informational text to teach students cause-effect relationships. When students complete the Plot/Concept Relationships chart, they are visually representing the connections between characters in stories, events in history, hierarchical concepts in science, or steps of inquiry in science.

Text Type
Narrative
Informational

When to Use
After Reading

Strategy
Monitoring Meaning
Inferring
Determining Importance
Synthesizing

How to Use
Individual

Procedure

1. To teach plot relationships, choose a story that has clear elements of plot such as characters, goal, problem, and solution. To teach cause-effect relationships, choose an informational text that has clear examples of events that lead to other events, for example, the events leading to Haiti's independence from France. To teach scientific concepts or steps of inquiry, choose a science text that has clear conceptual definitions or that states procedural steps of inquiry.

2. Use an example you develop or the sample Plot Relationships chart on page 84 to model for students how to use the strategy.

3. Display and duplicate copies of the Plot/Concept Relationships reproducible master on page 85 or adapt it to suit your needs or purposes.

4. To model plot relationships, review with students the basic elements of a story; that is, stories usually have main characters, a goal the characters wish to achieve, problems that prevent them from achieving the goal, and a solution to the problem. In the sample Plot Relationships chart, a story from a middle school literature anthology is used.

5. Read through the four boxes in the sample with students. Ask them to generate full sentences using the information in all four boxes. For example, "Carlos wanted to buy a new camera lens, but he did not have enough money, so he had to work more hours to earn the money."

6. Instruct students to read the story you chose for them and to use the strategy to first complete the four boxes. Then have students write out the complete sentence containing the basic information.

7. To model concept relationships, review with students how to determine cause and effect by looking for key words such as *because, when,* and *if-then.* See the sample Plot Relationships chart on page 84. In addition, see the website for Concept Relationships charts from middle school social studies and science texts.

8. Read through the four boxes in the sample with students and then ask them to generate full sentences using the information in all four boxes. For example, in the science sample, "Because humans are warm-blooded and breathe by lungs and sharks are cold-blooded and breathe by gills, humans are different from sharks."

9. Move on to the informational text you chose for the students. Instruct students to use the strategy to first complete the four boxes and then write out the complete sentence.

10. Demonstrate another type of Concept Relationships chart with headings of "Problem," "Hypothesis," "Testing," and "Conclusion." This sample chart is shown on the website. Discuss with students when this chart would be more appropriate for use than the other type of chart. For example, when a question is posed in science, this second chart is more appropriate. When a cause and effect relationship is delineated, the first chart is more appropriate.

11. Encourage students to use a Plot/Concept Relationships chart whenever they need to demonstrate comprehension of text. Reproducibles can be found on pages 85–86.

Reference

Schmidt, B., & Buckley, M. (1991). Plot relationships chart. In J. M. Macon, D. Bewell, & M. Vogt (Eds.), *Responses to literature: Grades K–8* (pp. 7–8). Newark, DE: International Reading Association.

Sample Plot Relationships for Middle School Literature

Somebody	Wanted	But	So
Carlos	to buy a new camera lens	he didn't have enough money	he had to work more hours to earn the money.

Carlos wanted to buy a new camera lens, but he didn't have enough money, so he had to work more hours to earn the money.

Plot/Concept Relationships

Somebody	Wanted	But	So

_____
_____
_____
_____
_____
_____
_____
_____

Concept Relationships

Problem	Hypothesis	Testing	Conclusion

_____

_____

_____

_____

_____

_____

_____

Possible Sentences

Focus
Vocabulary
Response

Text Type
Narrative
Informational

When to Use
Before Reading
After Reading

Strategy
Using Prior Knowledge
Inferring
Synthesizing

How to Use
Individual
Small Group
Whole Group

DESCRIPTION: The Possible Sentences strategy (Moore & Moore, 1992; Readence, Bean, & Baldwin, 2008) is used to help students predict the content in a selection and then check their predictions while reading. After reading, students use the text to support the accuracy of their predictions or revise them so they are more reflective of the content. The Possible Sentences strategy helps students set a purpose for reading and develop interest in and curiosity about the text. Through the use of the strategy, students formulate questions that they wish to answer by reading, make connections to their background knowledge, and, based on the vocabulary selected, make inferences about the content of the selection.

Procedure

1. Display 10–15 key vocabulary words (some new, some familiar) from a text selection and pronounce the words for the students.

2. Ask students to select at least two words from the list and use them in a sentence that they believe might reflect the content of the selection. Stress that students should use their prior knowledge about the words. Perhaps these words remind them of something they know about. Encourage them to write their sentences in the space provided on the reproducible master.

3. Ask students to share their sentences orally. Write them on the board as they are given, underlining words from the list. Continue until all the words have been used or until the available time has elapsed.

4. Have students read the text selection.

5. After reading, have students reread each sentence and determine its accuracy. Rate it **T** (true), **F** (false), or **DK** (don't know—not enough information given). Revise or omit those sentences that are not accurate and those about which insufficient information was provided in the text. Encourage students to cite specific text references in making their conclusions about sentence accuracy. After the sentences are corrected or verified to be correct, students could be asked to enter them into their notebooks or class log books.

6. An example for middle school social studies can be found on the following page. A reproducible is on page 89.

References

Moore, D. W., & Moore, S. A. (1992). Possible sentences: An update. In E. K. Dishner, T. W. Bean, J. E. Readence, & D. W. Moore (Eds.), *Reading in the content areas: Improving classroom instruction* (3rd ed.) (pp. 196–202). Dubuque, IA: Kendall Hunt.

Readence, J. E., Bean, T. W., & Baldwin, R. S. (2008). *Content area literacy: An integrated approach* (9th ed.). Dubuque, IA: Kendall Hunt.

Sample Possible Sentences for Middle School Social Studies

<u>Ancient Rome</u>
(topic)

Below are some words that you will find in your reading.

republic	*aqueduct*	*disciple*
dictator	*persecute*	*census*
veto	*martyr*	
forum	*legion*	

Possible Sentences

Directions: Write one or more sentences using at least two of the above terms in each sentence. Underline the words from the list above. After reading, rate the accuracy of each sentence by indicating True (T), False (F), or Don't Know (DK).

F 1. *One citizen became a <u>martyr</u> when he sacrificed his life rather than carry out the commands of the <u>dictator</u>.*

T 2. *The members of the <u>forum</u> conducted a <u>census</u> of the population to determine the ages and locations of everyone in the <u>republic</u>.*

DK 3. *Some of the members of the <u>legion</u> supported the building of an <u>aqueduct</u> to bring needed water to the town.*

Key

T = True

F = False, needs to be rewritten

DK = Don't know, information not given in the reading

Possible Sentences

_____
(topic)

Below are some words that you will find in your reading.

_____   _____   _____

_____   _____   _____

_____   _____   _____

_____   _____   _____

Possible Sentences

Directions: Write one or more sentences using at least two of the above terms in each sentence. Underline the words from the list above. After reading, rate the accuracy of each sentence by indicating True (T), False (F), or Don't Know (DK).

_____ 1. _____

_____

_____ 2. _____

_____

_____ 3. _____

_____

_____ 4. _____

_____

_____ 5. _____

_____

Key

T   = True

F   = False, needs to be rewritten

DK = Don't know, information not given in the reading

Question-Answer Relationships (QARs)

Focus
Comprehension

Text Type
Narrative
Informational

When to Use
After Reading

Strategy
Monitoring Meaning
Using Prior Knowledge
Asking Questions
Inferring
Creating Images
Determining Importance
Synthesizing

How to Use
Individual

DESCRIPTION: Question-Answer Relationships (Raphael, Highfield, & Au, 2006) help students to determine where and how to find answers to questions. There are two main categories of questions: *in the book QARs* and *in my head QARs*. The two "in the book" questions, "right there" and "putting it together," have answers supplied by the author. The two "in my head" questions, "author and me" and "on my own," have answers either partially or entirely based on students' knowledge and experiences (Buehl, 2009). Raphael and Pearson (1982) found that students in grades four, six, and eight who were taught the QAR strategy were more successful at answering questions than those students who were not taught the strategy. QARs are valuable for helping students to make the transition from explicitly stated information in texts to the often implicitly stated information found in more advanced reading materials.

Procedure

1. Ask students how they find information when they are asked to answer comprehension questions after reading an assignment. Discuss the various ways they cope with the challenge of answering difficult questions. Also, highlight just what it is that makes the questions difficult. For example, are they difficult because the information is not readily available? Or are they difficult because students must formulate their own conclusions? Use this discussion to introduce QARs.

2. Duplicate copies of the Question-Answer Relationships (QARs) reproducible master on page 94 or adapt it to suit your needs or purposes. Explain to students that as they progress through school, the types of questions they will be expected to answer become more challenging partly because the answers can come from a variety of places. You may want to display the reproducibles on pages 94 and 95 to help introduce the types of QARs.

3. Read aloud to students the sample passage on page 93 or white out the answers and distribute a sheet to each student. You could also use an example from your curriculum. Then model for students how you decide where to find the answers. If the questions are explicitly from the text, they are "right there" questions. Invite a student to show in the passage where the answer can be found. If the questions can be answered by using information from several places in the text, they are "putting it together" questions. Invite a student to show where connections in the passage can be made. If the questions involve looking for clues the author may have given, they are "author and me" questions. Invite a student to point out clues the author has given in the passage. And finally, if the questions require students to use their own knowledge and experiences, they are "on my own" questions. Model for students how to base answers on their own experiences and knowledge. Students may not agree with all the answers on page 93. You may also want to use the large visuals from the website for the four types of QARs.

4. Prepare a short text passage that contains information that you can use to create the four types of QAR questions. Include one or two of each type of question on the page. Either reproduce this passage for students or display it. You will use this passage when the students are ready to try the strategy on their own.

5. Prepare some questions to practice QARs. Instruct students to first read the passage silently, then identify the nature of each question asked after the passage. You may also wish to have students actually answer the questions. Take time to allow students to share their opinions about the types of questions asked and discuss how they decided the types of questions.

6. Distribute copies of the QAR reproducible. Instruct students to refer to it whenever they are asked to answer questions after reading and ask them to put the initials of the question type by each of their written answers. For example, if the question is "right there," students will write *RT* next to their answer. A suggested key is below.

   RT = Right There

   PIT = Putting It Together

   AAM = Author and Me

   OMO = On My Own

7. In subsequent lessons, help students understand that QARs can help them know where they will get information to answer questions in their reading.

8. Additional reproducibles can be found on the website.

References

Buehl, D. (2009). *Classroom strategies for interactive learning* (3rd ed.). Newark, DE: International Reading Association.

Raphael, T. E., Highfield, K., & Au, K. H. (2006). *QAR now: A powerful and practical framework that develops comprehension and higher-level thinking in all students.* New York: Scholastic.

Raphael, T. E., & Pearson, P. D. (1982). *The effect of metacognitive training on children's question-answering behavior.* Urbana, IL: Center for the Study of Reading.

Sample Question-Answer Relationships (QARs) for Middle School *Science*

The Life Sciences

Careers in life sciences can be divided into two major groups: the biology professions and the health professions. The professions in biology include many kinds of specialists who are involved in research and teaching. In general, entrance into these careers requires many years of college training plus original research.

Most biologists who study animals specialize in one group. For example, scientists called ichthyologists study fish, entomologists study insects, and herpetologists study reptiles and amphibians. Anatomists and physiologists study the structure of living organisms and the functioning of their bodies. Cytologists are biologists who study cells.

1. What do most biologists do in addition to teaching? (Answer: PIT)

Right There   **Putting It Together**   **Author and Me**   **On My Own**

2. What are the two major groups of careers in life sciences? (Answer: RT)

Right There   **Putting It Together**   **Author and Me**   **On My Own**

3. How many years must one go to college to be a biologist? (Answer: OMO)

Right There   **Putting It Together**   **Author and Me**   **On My Own**

4. What is the suffix, or word ending, used to describe careers in biology? (Answer: AAM)

Right There   **Putting It Together**   **Author and Me**   **On My Own**

Question-Answer Relationships (QARs)

Right There

Putting It Together

Author and Me

On My Own

In The Book Questions

Right There: The answer to the question is right in the book. You can look for key words to help you find the answer.

Putting It Together: The answer is in the book, but not as easy to find. You may have to combine pieces of information from different places in the book.

In My Head Questions

Author and Me: The author may have given hints or clues that you combine with what you know to help you to figure out the answer.

On My Own: The answer is in your head. These are the questions that you really have to take time to think through. You may have to think about what you already know or about experiences you've had.

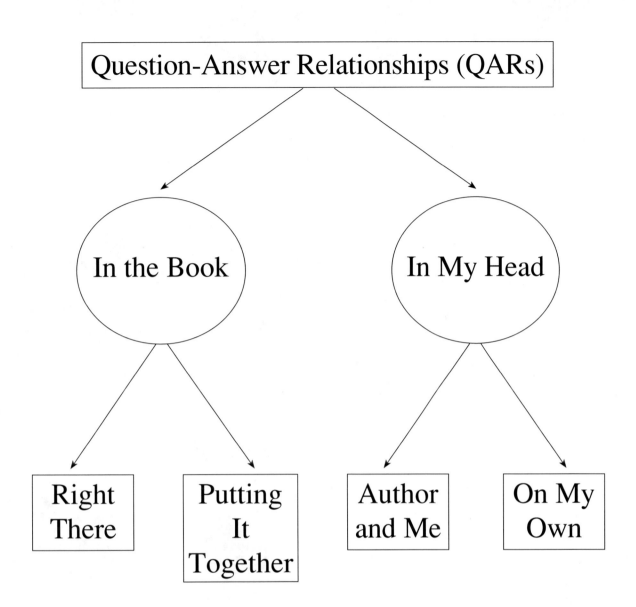

Question-Answer Relationships (QARs)

In the Book

In My Head

Right There

Putting It Together

Author and Me

On My Own

Role, Audience, Format, Topic (RAFT)

Focus
Response

Text Type
Narrative
Informational

When to Use
After Reading

Strategy
Inferring
Determining Importance
Synthesizing

How to Use
Individual

DESCRIPTION: RAFT (Role, Audience, Format, Topic) (Santa, Havens, & Valdes, 2004) is a strategy that is useful in all content areas. It encourages students to write from a perspective or viewpoint other than their own and in a form that may be more unusual than common. The purpose is to provide opportunities for students to demonstrate their understanding of a topic or subject through a writing experience that helps them to think about the subject and communicate their understanding of it in a creative and sometimes entertaining and interesting way. RAFT writing assignments often motivate students to write in an in-depth and organized fashion and, in the process, help them to think about and more fully understand the subject being studied.

Procedure

1. Consider the major concepts of the chapter, unit, or selection being used in your classroom.

2. Consider possible roles that students might assume. For example, if the class is studying Ancient Rome, possible roles might be a gladiator's sword, a member of the tribunal or senate, a Roman general, a chariot, or a Roman coin.

3. Decide on possible audiences, formats, and topics for the assignment that might help students extend their understanding of what the class is studying. For example, if Ancient Rome is the topic, audiences might be slave owners, mercenary soldiers, tourists, or citizens of Rome. Formats might be a newspaper editorial, a journal entry, a speech, an advertisement, a travel brochure, or a eulogy. Possible topics might include discouraging violence in Rome, proposing cooperation with another government, justifying service in the Roman army, conducting a guided tour of Ancient Rome, or possibly mourning the death of the Roman empire.

4. Prepare a RAFT assignment for your students listing the possible roles, audiences, formats, and topics they might use. Possible examples of RAFT assignments are found on pages 100–101.

5. Present the concept of RAFT to your students, including its four components, and share some examples with them. (See the RAFT examples on pages 98 and 99).

6. Have students choose their roles and then work in small groups with students who have selected the same role to brainstorm possible information and emotions that might be shared through the role of the writer.

7. Finally, have students select their audience, format, and topic and begin work.

8. Because RAFT assignments vary a great deal, it is helpful to share a rubric for grading the work at the outset so that students understand the criteria on which they will be judged. Areas of the rubric might include: writing was appropriate for intended audience; writing followed chosen format; information presented was accurate; grammar and mechanics were acceptable.

Selected areas can be weighted for greater emphasis. Be sure to star (*) these areas on the reproducible master before reproducing it.

9. As students gain greater competence with RAFT, they can help determine what to use for the four RAFT elements (Role, Audience, Format, Topic).

Reference

Santa, C. M., Havens, L. T., & Valdes, B. J. (2004). *Project CRISS: Creating independence through student-owned strategies* (3rd ed.). Dubuque, IA: Kendall Hunt.

Sample RAFT Assignment for Intermediate Grade Students Studying the **Revolutionary War**

Directions: Consider the RAFT possibilities listed below. Choose your role and circle it. Now discuss that role with others who have selected the same one. Consider the following in your discussion.

1. Describe me.
2. What feelings do I have?
3. What information do I need to convey through my writing?
4. What words or ideas might I include to get my point across?
5. What do I know about my audience? What type of information or persuasion might they need?
6. What do I already know about the format? How might it look?

Role	Audience	Format	Topic
Young Colonist Boy	Sons of Liberty	Resume	Wants to Join
Paul Revere's Horse	Other War Horses	Memo	The Midnight Ride
Patriot Soldier	Your Family	Letter Home	Reality of War
Colonist	King	Speech	Stop Unfair Taxation
Tea	Colonists	Editorial	Stop Boston Tea Party
News Reporter	Future Generations	News Release	Tell Why Boston Massacre Was Significant
American Flag	British Citizens	Poem	Freedom

When you have finished your discussion, you may begin your work. Your RAFT assignment should be at least one page in length and will be judged using the following criteria. The starred (*) items are worth double points.

Completed on Time	1	2	3	4	5
Writing Appropriate for Audience*	1	2	3	4	5
Format Followed	1	2	3	4	5
Information Accurate*	1	2	3	4	5
Grammar and Mechanics	1	2	3	4	5
Neatness	1	2	3	4	5
Creativity	1	2	3	4	5

Sample RAFT Assignment for Middle School Students Studying **Ancient Greece**

Directions: Consider the RAFT possibilities listed below. Choose your role and circle it. Now discuss that role with others who have selected the same one. Consider the following in your discussion.

1. Describe me.
2. What feelings do I have?
3. What information do I need to convey through my writing?
4. What words or ideas might I include to get my point across?
5. What do I know about my audience? What type of information or persuasion might they need?
6. What do I already know about the format? How might it look?

Role	Audience	Format	Topic
Socrates	The Athenian Court	Plea	Spare His Life
Alexander's Sword	Self	Diary	Living with Alexander the Great
Corinthian Column	Greek Architects	Resume	Job Application
Hermes	Zeus	Letter	Work Overload
Letter F	Greek Alphabet	Memo	Wishes to Join the Greek Alphabet
Grapes and Olives	Tourists	Travel Brochure	Visit Greece
Ship	Greek Traders	Advertisement	Hire Me

When you have finished your discussion, you may begin your work. Your RAFT assignment should be at least one page in length and will be judged using the following criteria. The starred (*) items are worth double points.

Completed on Time*	1	2	3	4	5
Writing Appropriate for Audience	1	2	3	4	5
Format Followed*	1	2	3	4	5
Information Accurate*	1	2	3	4	5
Grammar and Mechanics	1	2	3	4	5
Neatness	1	2	3	4	5
Creativity	1	2	3	4	5

Sample RAFT Assignments

Role	Audience	Format	Topic
Sue, the T-Rex Dinosaur	Paleontologist	Memoir	Life in the Time of Dinosaurs
Newspaper Columnist	Jury	Testimonial	Freedom of Speech
Flight Attendant	Pilots	Proposal	Equal Pay
Chef	Cooking Class	Instructions	How to Create the Perfect Meal
Semicolon	High School Students	Complaint Letter	How It Is Misused
Meteorologist	Hurricanes	Statistics	How They Compare
Student Body President	Principal	Proposal	Reasons Why Longer Lunch Hour Needed
Naturalist John Muir	Lumber Industry	Commercial	Conservation of Natural Resources
Michelangelo	Pope	Bill	Services Provided during Painting of Sistine Chapel
Salmon	Grand Coulee Dam	Flyer	Difficulties Caused by Dam
Fraction	Whole Number	Letter	How They Are Different How They Should Work Together
Soil	Earthworm	Menu	Soil Varieties
Blood	Doctor	Travelogue	Movement through Body
Triangle	Mathematician	Appeal	Why It Is Needed
Muscles	Treadmill	Love Letter	Benefits of Exercise
Plant	Water	Thank You Note	Benefits of Water
Harry Potter	Children	Poem	The Wonders of Wizardry
Basketball	New Player	Advice Column	Tips for Success
Auctioneer	Customers	List	Paintings for Sale
Self	Book Character	Yearbook Inscription	Best Character Traits

From Jerry L. Johns and Roberta L. Berglund, *Strategies for Content Area Learning* (3rd ed.). Copyright © 2011 by Kendall Hunt Publishing Company (1-800-247-3458, ext. 4). May be reproduced for noncommercial educational purposes. www.kendallhunt.com/readingresources

Sample RAFT Assignments

Role	Audience	Format	Topic
Book Character	Another character in the book	Letter	Ask for suggestions for solving the problem in the story
Main Character	Students	Advice Column	Ask for help solving the conflict in the story
Animal in Rainforest	General Public	Letter to the Editor	Saving the Rainforest
Big Foot	General Public	Letter/News Story	Why I really exist
Cell Organelle	Boss/Employee	Resume	What I can do for the cell
MRNA	Parents/Friends	Letter from Camp	Describe protein synthesis
Teacher	Incoming Students	Letter	Advice
Greek God	Other Gods	Letter	Opinions on what is happening from the poem
Reporter	Public—Choose either a Northern or Southern Perspective	Newspaper	Events leading up to the Civil War (i.e., Bleeding Kansas, John Brown)
Sec/csc/cot	Calculator Company	Letter	Reasons to get own button on calculator
Pencil	Math Teacher	Recipe	Steps to solve a word problem
Teacher	Little Brother, Sister, or Parent	Lesson (conversation and dialogues)	Teach the concept of inertia

From Jerry L. Johns and Roberta L. Berglund, *Strategies for Content Area Learning* (3rd ed.). Copyright © 2011 by Kendall Hunt Publishing Company (1-800-247-3458, ext. 4). May be reproduced for noncommercial educational purposes. www.kendallhunt.com/readingresources

RAFT

Directions: Consider the RAFT possibilities listed below. Choose your role and circle it. Now discuss that role with others who have selected the same one. Consider the following in your discussion.

1. Describe me.
2. What feelings do I have?
3. What information do I need to convey through my writing?
4. What words or ideas might I include to get my point across?
5. What do I know about my audience? What type of information or persuasion might they need?
6. What do I already know about the format? How might it look?

Role	Audience	Format	Topic

When you have finished your discussion, you may begin your work. Your RAFT assignment should be at least one page in length and will be judged using the following criteria. The starred (*) items are worth double points.

Completed on Time	1	2	3	4	5
Writing Appropriate for Audience	1	2	3	4	5
Format Followed	1	2	3	4	5
Information Accurate	1	2	3	4	5
Grammar and Mechanics	1	2	3	4	5
Neatness	1	2	3	4	5
Creativity	1	2	3	4	5

Save the Last Word for Me

DESCRIPTION: Save the Last Word for Me (Short, Harste, & Burke, 1996; Vaughan & Estes, 1986) is a useful strategy in all content areas. With this strategy, students are encouraged to take an active role in selecting and responding to sections of a text that they find interesting or about which they have a reaction. They then have an opportunity to discuss their choices with other students. One of the advantages of Save the Last Word for Me is that everyone has an opportunity to comment before the student who shares the quote comments about it. This procedure allows the student to consider additional ideas and to add to or delete ideas from his or her original response prior to sharing it with others.

Procedure

1. Distribute three 3x5-inch cards to each student or make copies of the Save the Last Word for Me reproducible master on page 105 and distribute one to each student.

2. Have each student read the selected text independently.

3. As students read, have them lightly mark with pencil sentences or small sections of the text about which they have a reaction, question, or connection.

4. After reading, have students select three of the sentences or sections of text they have marked and write each on an index card or on their copy of the Save the Last Word for Me reproducible.

5. Students then need to write their comments and thoughts about each of the text segments on the back of the cards or on the Save the Last Word for Me reproducible. When this task is completed, place students in groups of 4 or 5. You may want to display the Discussion Guide on page 106 and use it to highlight the procedures that follow. The Discussion Guide can also be referred to as students share.

6. Choose one student in each group to begin. That student reads one of the text segments he or she has selected. Only the text segment is shared at this time.

7. Each member of the group is then invited to comment on the first student's text segment or quote.

8. When all students in the group have commented, then the student who shared the quote offers his or her comments about it. The comments may or may not be the same as the original thoughts or ideas that were written.

9. The process continues by having another student share a quote from one of the cards or the Save the Last Word for Me reproducible.

10. At the conclusion of the lesson, ask students if selecting the sentences and discussing them helped them understand the text. Stress that making connections, asking questions, and reacting during reading can aid students' understanding of the selection. A completed sample is provided on page 104.

References

Short, K. G., Harste, J. C., & Burke, C. (1996). *Creating classrooms for authors and inquirers* (2nd ed.). Portsmouth, NH: Heinemann.

Vaughan, J. L., & Estes, T. H. (1986). *Reading and reasoning beyond the primary grades*. Boston: Allyn & Bacon.

Focus
Response

Text Type
Narrative
Informational

When to Use
During Reading
After Reading

Strategy
Using Prior Knowledge
Asking Questions
Inferring
Determining Importance
Synthesizing

How to Use
Individual
Small Group

Sample Save the Last Word for Me for High School **Health**

Directions: As you read, make a light mark with your pencil next to three (3) statements in the passage that you either agree with, disagree with, connect with, or wish to comment about. When you finish reading, write each statement in one of the boxes below. Then write your comments below it. You might include questions or thoughts you have about each of the quotes. When you have finished, you will have an opportunity to discuss your comments with a small group of your classmates.

Title: _Coping with Loss_

My First Quote, page _228_

Any loss requires change and that change can be stressful.

My Thoughts/Ideas/Questions about My First Quote

Change is hard when you don't choose it. That's what makes it stressful.

My Second Quote, page _229_

Hope operates through all five stages of grief.

My Thoughts/Ideas/Questions about My Second Quote

I think this is helpful to remember, especially when I am trying to help my girlfriend get over being hurt.

My Third Quote, page _230_

What helped me most was talking to my family.

My Thoughts/Ideas/Questions about My Third Quote

When my grandma died, it seemed that the only time I felt better was when I could be with my family and tell them how awful I was feeling.

Save the Last Word for Me

Directions: As you read, make a light mark with your pencil next to three (3) statements in the passage that you either agree with, disagree with, connect with, or wish to comment about. When you finish reading, write each statement in one of the boxes below. Then write your comments below it. You might include questions or thoughts you have about each of the quotes. When you have finished, you will have an opportunity to discuss your comments with a small group of your classmates.

Title: _____

My First Quote, page _____

My Thoughts/Ideas/Questions about My First Quote

My Second Quote, page _____

My Thoughts/Ideas/Questions about My Second Quote

My Third Quote, page _____

My Thoughts/Ideas/Questions about My Third Quote

Based on Short, Harste, and Burke (1996) and Vaughan and Estes (1986). From Jerry L. Johns and Roberta L. Berglund, *Strategies for Content Area Learning* (3rd ed.). Copyright © 2011 by Kendall Hunt Publishing Company (1-800-247-3458, ext. 4). May be reproduced for noncommercial educational purposes. www.kendallhunt.com/readingresources

1 Choose someone to begin.

2 Have the first person read his or her first quote, but make no comment about it.

3 Moving around the circle, have each member of the group take a turn in commenting about the first person's quote.

4 When each person has had a chance to comment, the person who chose the quote may then share his or her comment about the quote. This may be a combination of what was written on the card as well as a response to what was said during the discussion.

5 Select another member of the group to read a quote.

6 Continue the reading and commenting until all quotes and comments have been made.

7 Remember that the person who shares a quote needs to be the **last** one to make comments about it. In other words, "Save the last word for me!"

Say Something

DESCRIPTION: Say Something (Short, Harste, & Burke, 1996) provides opportunities for students to respond to text. The strategy highlights the social nature of language by offering students the opportunity to share their thinking with a partner. At pre-selected stopping points in the reading, students make connections between the text and their own experiences and briefly discuss what the passage means to them. When using Say Something, students engage in proficient reader strategies by chunking text, posing questions, making predictions, and highlighting connections. Through the use of Say Something, students become more engaged in reading and aware of effective strategies to use when reading independently.

Focus
Response

Text Type
Narrative
Informational

When to Use
During Reading

Strategy
Using Prior Knowledge
Asking Questions
Inferring
Synthesizing

How to Use
Small Group

Procedure

1. Select a reading passage and stopping points within the passage. Paragraphs and sections of text with subheadings make good stopping points.

2. Invite students to choose a partner or designate partners.

3. Give each partner pair a copy of the text selection.

4. Invite each partner pair to decide how they will read the selection, silently or aloud.

5. To introduce the strategy, demonstrate the Say Something process with another student, using the first segment or two of the selected text.

6. When students appear to understand how to engage in the process, invite students to read to the next stopping point and Say Something to their partner about what they have read. Suggestions to help students successfully participate in Say Something are found on page 108. Emphasize that responses and interpretations are acceptable if the student can support the position.

7. When students finish the selection, conduct a discussion of the process. Create a list of the strategies students used while engaging in this strategy. Help students understand how they can use the strategies of using prior knowledge, questioning, inferring, and synthesizing when they are reading independently.

Reference

Short, K. G., Harste, J. C., & Burke, C. (1996). *Creating classrooms for authors and inquirers* (2nd ed.). Portsmouth, NH: Heinemann.

Say Something

When working with your partner, you might select from the following ideas to form your comments.

- That reminds me of . . .
- I can relate to . . .
- I'm thinking . . .
- I'm wondering . . .
- I am confused about . . .
- I don't understand . . .
- What if . . .
- Perhaps . . .
- I think . . .
- I infer . . .
- It could mean . . .
- Now I understand why . . .
- I used to think _____ , but now I think _____

Say Something

When working with your partner, you might select from the following ideas to form your comments.

- That reminds me of . . .
- I can relate to . . .
- I'm thinking . . .
- I'm wondering . . .
- I am confused about . . .
- I don't understand . . .
- What if . . .
- Perhaps . . .
- I think . . .
- I infer . . .
- It could mean . . .
- Now I understand why . . .
- I used to think _____ , but now I think _____

From Jerry L. Johns and Roberta L. Berglund, *Strategies for Content Area Learning* (3rd ed.). Copyright © 2011 by Kendall Hunt Publishing Company (1-800-247-3458, ext. 4). May be reproduced for noncommercial educational purposes. www.kendallhunt.com/readingresources

Select Two and Reflect (STAR)

DESCRIPTION: Students are asked to choose two words from a selection that they have read and then explain in writing why those particular words were selected (Hoyt, 2008). Select Two and Reflect (STAR) encourages diverse thinking, honors individual responses, and invites students to react to words in a way that is personal and meaningful.

Procedure

1. Duplicate copies of the Select Two and Reflect (STAR) reproducible master on page 111 or adapt it to suit your needs or purposes.

2. Ask students to review a selection or passage that has been read and to identify two interesting words. Do not, at this time, suggest any particular criteria for selecting the words.

3. After students have selected their words, ask for volunteers to share their words as you write them on the board.

4. Ask students to share why particular words were selected. Guide students to understand that some words were chosen because they were important in the selection. Other words were chosen because they reminded students of something in their lives, and sometimes words were selected because they were interesting in sound or possessed some other quality. An example is given on page 110.

5. Distribute copies of the STAR sheet to students after they have read a particular selection. Have students review the selection and write a word in each box. Then give students a few minutes to write why the words were selected.

6. Invite students to share their words and reasons in groups of three students.

7. Encourage whole group sharing after students have shared in their small groups. Expect and reinforce both the variety of words selected and the students' reasons for choosing them.

8. Model the process from time to time by completing a STAR sheet while students are completing theirs. Share your words and reasons with a small group of students or with the entire class.

Reference

Hoyt, L. (2008). *Revisit, reflect, retell: Time-tested strategies for teaching reading comprehension.* Portsmouth, NH: Heinemann.

Focus
Vocabulary
Comprehension
Response

Text Type
Narrative
Informational

When to Use
After Reading

Strategy
Using Prior Knowledge
Creating Images
Determining Importance

How to Use
Individual
Small Group
Whole Group

Sample Select Two and Reflect (STAR) for Middle School Language Arts

Directions: Choose two words from the selection and explain why you chose them. You can also explain how they relate to your reading or your life.

Title: *"Cheating Mr. Diskin"*

money	*dirt*
Word 1	Word 2

Why Words Were Chosen

I chose money because the boys needed it to go to the show. They got the money by cheating. When they went to the show, they felt like dirt. Dirt is really low.

Select Two and Reflect (STAR)

Directions: Choose two words from the selection and explain why you chose them. You can also explain how they relate to your reading or your life.

Title: _____

<table>
<tr><td></td><td></td></tr>
<tr><td>Word 1</td><td>Word 2</td></tr>
</table>

Why Words Were Chosen

_____

_____

_____

_____

_____

_____

_____

_____

Selective Reading Guide

DESCRIPTION: The Selective Reading Guide (Cunningham & Shabloak, 1975) models for students how to identify important information in content area texts. Students are taught how mature readers make decisions about what to focus on while they read. Some portions of texts require more careful reading than other portions. The Selective Reading Guide strengthens students' abilities to be flexible in their reading (Tierney & Readence, 2005).

Procedure

1. Duplicate copies of the Selective Reading Guide reproducible master on page 115. You may wish to adapt it to suit your needs or purposes.

2. Select a passage from a content area text that is new to your students.

3. Identify the concepts you want your students to master by reading the passage; that is, what should they know and what should they be able to do after the reading?

4. Display a page within the passage that includes examples of textual cues indicating importance, such as words in bold print or italics, subheadings, and words printed in different colors. You may wish to enlarge the copy of the passage to permit easier reading. Also consider highlighting the words that were in different colors in the original text. (See the reproducible master on page 115 for a more thorough list of cues.)

5. Discuss with students the kinds of difficulties they encounter when they attempt to thoroughly read content area texts. For example, they may describe their frustration in being unable to absorb all the information in the reading assignment or indicate it is difficult to stay focused when assignments are lengthy.

6. Distribute copies of the Selective Reading Guide. Explain to students that they are to self-monitor their reading by checking off the important characteristics as they find them.

7. Using the passage and the Selective Reading Guide, read the passage or selection aloud and model for students how to attend to the important features in the text. For example, if you are modeling how to read a social studies text, show the students how to look for key dates, names, and places and tell them that generally the text will explain their importance either in the same sentence or in the following sentence. If you are modeling how to read a science text, demonstrate how to find the steps or stages the text describes by searching for words such as *first, next,* or *finally*. You may also wish to point out cause and effect words such as *because* and *therefore*. Also model how students may self-monitor their use of the Selective Reading Guide by checking off the steps as they complete them.

8. Direct students' attention to the assigned reading. Instruct students to silently read the passage and as they read to watch for the important features they have learned to identify. Also remind students to check off the steps of the strategy as they complete them.

Focus
Vocabulary
Comprehension

Text Type
Informational

When to Use
During Reading

Strategy
Monitoring Meaning
Inferring
Determining Importance

How to Use
Individual

9. When students are finished reading, ask for their feedback on the strategy. Discuss the situations for which this strategy would be most appropriate.

10. An additional example can be found on the website.

References

Cunningham, R., & Shabloak, S. (1975). Selective reading guide-o-rama: The content teacher's best friend. *Journal of Reading,* *18,* 380–382.

Tierney, R. J., & Readence, J. E. (2005). *Reading strategies and practices: A compendium* (6th ed.). Boston: Allyn & Bacon.

Sample Selective Reading Guide for *Social Studies*

___✓___ I read the **HEADINGS** of the chapter sections and referred to them while I read the passage to help me remember the purpose of the reading.

___✓___ I read the **Subheadings** in the chapter and referred to them while I read to help me remember what each section was about.

___✓___ I paid special attention to words in color, in **bold print**, and in *italics*, and I watched for the meanings of those words in the sentences.

___✓___ I looked for key listing words such as *first, next,* and *because* to help me find important sequences of events or procedural steps to follow.

___✓___ I looked for proper nouns such as names of events, procedures, people, or places to help me know which are most important to recall.

Headings I Read

Africa's Climates

Subheadings I Read

Different Climate Zones, Tropical Rain Forest Climate, Tropical Wet-and-Dry
Climate, Steppe Climate, Desert Climate, Mediterranean Climate

Words in Color, Bold Print, <u>Underlined</u>, or in *Italics*	**Meanings**
tropical rain forest climate	hot and rainy
tropical wet-and-dry climate	savannah, grassland
steppe climate	hot summers, cool winters
desert climate	extremely hot days, chilly nights (Sahara)
Mediterranean climate	cool & rainy winter, warm & dry summer

Sequence of Events or Procedural Steps to Follow

None

Key Events, Procedures, People, Places, and Their Significance

Madagascar—tropical rain forest climate

Zambia—savannah

Sahara, Horn, Kalahari, & Namib—African deserts

Selective Reading Guide

Title _____ Pages _____

_____ I read the **<u>HEADINGS</u>** of the chapter sections and referred to them while I read the passage to help me remember the purpose of the reading.

_____ I read the **Subheadings** in the chapter and referred to them while I read to help me remember what each section was about.

_____ I paid special attention to words in color, in **bold print**, and in *italics*, and I watched for the meanings of those words in the sentences.

_____ I looked for key listing words such as *first, next,* and *because* to help me find important sequences of events or procedural steps to follow.

_____ I looked for proper nouns such as names of events, procedures, people, or places to help me know which are most important to recall.

Headings I Read

_____

Subheadings I Read

_____

Words in Color, in Bold Print,
<u>Underlined</u>, or in *Italics*   **Meanings**

_____

_____

_____

_____

Sequence of Events or Procedural Steps to Follow

_____

Key Events, Procedures, People, Places, and Their Significance

_____

_____

_____

_____

_____

Based on Cunningham and Shabloak (1975). From Jerry L. Johns and Roberta L. Berglund, *Strategies for Content Area Learning* (3rd ed.). Copyright © 2011 by Kendall Hunt Publishing Company (1-800-247-3458, ext. 4). May be reproduced for noncommercial educational purposes. www.kendallhunt.com/readingresources

Self-Monitoring Approach to Reading and Thinking (SMART)

Focus
Comprehension

Text Type
Narrative
Informational

When to Use
During Reading
After Reading

Strategy
Monitoring Meaning
Asking Questions
Inferring

How to Use
Individual

DESCRIPTION: The Self-Monitoring Approach to Reading and Thinking (SMART) (Buehl, 2001; Vaughan & Estes, 1986) is a during-reading and after-reading strategy that encourages students to develop an awareness of what they do and do not understand as they read. This self-monitoring strategy helps students think about their reading to be more aware of how it is proceeding. Students use a notation system during reading and a variety of fix-up strategies for difficult portions of the text after reading, thus enhancing their metacognition (awareness of one's own learning).

Procedure

1. Find a passage consisting of several paragraphs that is somewhat challenging for you. The passage may need to be enlarged for effective viewing by students.

2. Read aloud the first few sentences of the passage. If it makes sense to you, place a check mark (✓) in the margin and say something like, "This makes sense to me. I feel like I really understand it." If it seems confusing, place a question mark (?) in the margin and say something like, "I'm not sure what this means. Maybe as I read on I will understand it better."

3. Continue modeling the use of the check mark (✓) and question mark (?) and comment on your reasons for using the marking system. You might say, "These marks will help me think about my reading and how well I am understanding what I am reading. Good readers know when they aren't understanding something, and they also know that they should try something else when they don't understand."

4. After completing the modeled reading for students, look at each question mark (?) and talk with students about how to make sense of those parts of the text. Sometimes just rereading the text helps a reader understand it. If this is the case for you, change the question mark (?) to a check mark (✓) in the margin. For other question-marked sections, talk about the problem. Why is this section difficult to understand? Is it the vocabulary? Is the language confusing? Do you know very little about the subject?

5. Ask students for their ideas of ways to help the text make sense. List these ideas on the board as students offer them. Suggestions might be to para-phrase the text, use pictures, charts, or graphs to give clues to understanding, check the glossary or other references to determine the meaning of unknown or difficult words, look at other parts of the text such as the summary and review sections, and ask a teacher or another classmate for help. Take time to discuss how the various strategies may provide clues to meaning.

6. Introduce the passage students will be reading. After using an appropriate rereading strategy (e.g., Anticipation/Reaction Guide on page 1, Possible Sentences on page 87, K-W-L Plus on page 71), tell students to use a pencil to lightly mark the text using the check mark (✓) and question mark (?) system to help them monitor their reading.

7. Make copies of the SMART Strategy Log reproducible master on page 120. After students have read and marked their passages, have them work with a partner and discuss the sections marked with question marks (?). Have them use the SMART Strategy Log to record their reading processes. Remind students that if the problem is "something else," there is space provided to note the problem.

8. After completing the SMART Strategy Log, discuss with students the strategies that helped them work through problems with the text. Review or teach what they need to do when they don't understand what they are reading in subsequent lessons.

9. Have students complete the SMART Strategy Log from time to time to help make them more aware of ways to monitor their comprehension. A completed SMART example is found on page 119.

References

Buehl, D. (2001). *Classroom strategies for interactive learning* (2nd ed.). Newark, DE: International Reading Association.

Vaughan, J. L., & Estes, T. H. (1986). *Reading and reasoning beyond the primary grades*. Boston: Allyn & Bacon.

Sample SMART Strategy Log for Intermediate Mathematics

Directions: After reading, find the page and paragraph of each question mark (?) in the margin of your text. Write them under the *Page/Paragraph* headings. Then look at each section of the text marked with a question mark (?). Ask yourself, *What's the Problem?* Check (✓) the things that may be problems or write your problem on the lines. Then try some fix-up strategies. Check (✓) those that you tried under the *What I Tried* column. Then think about how each strategy worked. Mark your responses in the *How It Worked* column with a check mark.

Page/Paragraph with "?"	What's the Problem?	What I Tried	How It Worked
	✓ Difficult Word Confusing Sentence Don't Know Much About It _____ _____	✓ Glossary Reread Text Pictures/Graphics Summarize Review Section Diagrams ✓ Ask Someone Something Else	Great! I Get It! ✓ It Helped OK Not Much Help
_36_ / _3_			

Page/Paragraph with "?"	What's the Problem?	What I Tried	How It Worked
	Difficult Word ✓ Confusing Sentence Don't Know Much About It _____ _____	Glossary ✓ Reread Text Pictures/Graphics Summarize Review Section Diagrams Ask Someone Something Else	✓ Great! I Get It! It Helped OK Not Much Help
_38_ / _1_			

Page/Paragraph with "?"	What's the Problem?	What I Tried	How It Worked
	Difficult Word ✓ Confusing Sentence Don't Know Much About It _____ _____	Glossary ✓ Reread Text ✓ Pictures/Graphics Summarize Review Section Diagrams Ask Someone Something Else	Great! I Get It! It Helped ✓ OK Not Much Help
_41_ / _2_			

Page/Paragraph with "?"	What's the Problem?	What I Tried	How It Worked
	Difficult Word Confusing Sentence ✓ Don't Know Much About It ✓ *Don't understand* _____	Glossary ✓ Reread Text ✓ Pictures/Graphics Summarize Review Section ✓ Diagrams Ask Someone Something Else	Great! I Get It! It Helped OK ✓ Not Much Help
_43_ / _2_			

SMART Strategy Log

Directions: After reading, find the page and paragraph of each question mark (?) in the margin of your text. Write them under the *Page/Paragraph* headings. Then look at each section of the text marked with a question mark (?). Ask yourself, *What's the Problem?* Check (✔) the things that may be problems or write your problem on the lines. Then try some fix-up strategies. Check (✔) those that you tried under the *What I Tried* column. Then think about how each strategy worked. Mark your responses in the *How It Worked* column with a check mark.

Page/Paragraph with "?"	*What's the Problem?*	*What I Tried*	*How It Worked*
	Difficult Word	Glossary	Great! I Get It!
	Confusing Sentence	Reread Text	It Helped
	Don't Know Much About It	Pictures/Graphics	OK
_____ / _____		Summarize	Not Much Help
	_____	Review Section	
		Diagrams	
	_____	Ask Someone	
		Something Else	

Page/Paragraph with "?"	*What's the Problem?*	*What I Tried*	*How It Worked*
	Difficult Word	Glossary	Great! I Get It!
	Confusing Sentence	Reread Text	It Helped
	Don't Know Much About It	Pictures/Graphics	OK
_____ / _____		Summarize	Not Much Help
	_____	Review Section	
		Diagrams	
	_____	Ask Someone	
		Something Else	

Page/Paragraph with "?"	*What's the Problem?*	*What I Tried*	*How It Worked*
	Difficult Word	Glossary	Great! I Get It!
	Confusing Sentence	Reread Text	It Helped
	Don't Know Much About It	Pictures/Graphics	OK
_____ / _____		Summarize	Not Much Help
	_____	Review Section	
		Diagrams	
	_____	Ask Someone	
		Something Else	

Page/Paragraph with "?"	*What's the Problem?*	*What I Tried*	*How It Worked*
	Difficult Word	Glossary	Great! I Get It!
	Confusing Sentence	Reread Text	It Helped
	Don't Know Much About It	Pictures/Graphics	OK
_____ / _____		Summarize	Not Much Help
	_____	Review Section	
		Diagrams	
	_____	Ask Someone	
		Something Else	

Semantic Feature Analysis (SFA)

DESCRIPTION: Semantic Feature Analysis (Berglund, 2002; Johnson & Pearson, 1984), is an instructional strategy that helps students discriminate the unique features of concepts or vocabulary. It uses a classification system in the form of a grid to help students determine semantic similarities and differences among closely related concepts.

Procedure

1. Display the reproducible master on page 123. Introduce the strategy by selecting a topic. It is best to introduce the SFA strategy to students by using a topic that is familiar to many of them, for example, Monsters.

2. List the words in the category down the left side of the grid. For the Monsters example, you might list *King Kong, Incredible Hulk, Dracula, Cookie Monster*, and *Godzilla*. Invite students to add additional monsters.

3. Across the top of the chart, list features shared by some of the words in the category. The features for Monsters might be *Hairy, Huge, Strong, Mean, Transforms*.

4. Consider each word in the category relative to the features listed across the top of the grid. A plus/minus (+/–) system or a numeric system (1 = never, 2 = some, 3 = always) can be used to indicate feature possession. If the presence of the feature may be situational or not dichotomous, the numerical rating system might be more useful. A question mark (?) can signal the need for more information. A plus/minus rating (+/–) indicates that the feature may be present in differing degrees or at various times. In the Monster example, King Kong would probably receive pluses (+) for the features, *Hairy, Huge, Strong*, and *Mean*, but would receive a minus (–) for *Transforms*. Students should be encouraged to discuss and provide support for their ratings.

5. Complete the grid for each word in the category. You may need to add more features to the matrix in order to discriminate the differences among some of the words in the category. For example, if two of the monsters in the example have an identical pattern of features (pluses and minuses), then additional features would need to be added until the difference between the two is discriminated.

6. When the grid is complete, ask students to examine the similarities and differences among the words in the category selected. Discuss some of their conclusions. Using the pattern of pluses and minuses, encourage students to create a summary statement regarding some of the words in the grid. For example, the summary of knowledge about Monsters might go something like this, "*King Kong, Dracula*, and *Godzilla* are all examples of monsters who are strong. Most monsters are huge, but not all monsters are mean."

7. If used before and after reading, a grid for that purpose is available on the website.

Focus
Vocabulary

Text Type
Narrative
Informational

When to Use
After Reading

Strategy
Asking Questions
Inferring
Synthesizing

How to Use
Individual
Small Group
Whole Group

References

Berglund, R. L. (2002). Semantic feature analysis. In B. J. Guzzetti (Ed.), *Literacy in America: An encyclopedia of history, theory, and practice* (pp. 566–572). Santa Barbara, CA: ABC-CLIO.

Johnson, D. D., & Pearson, P. D. (1984). *Teaching reading vocabulary* (2nd ed.). New York: Holt, Rinehart, and Winston.

Sample Semantic Feature Analysis (SFA) for High School Earth Science

Rivers and River Characteristics
(topic)

Words / Features	Caused by Erosion	Caused by Deposition	Old	Mature	Young					
Waterfalls	+	−	−	−	+					
Rapids	+	−	−	−	+					
Wide Flood Plain	+	+	+	+/−	−					
U-Shape Valley	+	−	−	−	+					
Meander	+	+	+	+	−					
Oxbow	+	−	+	−	−					
Yazoo Stream	−	+	+	−	−					
No Flood Plain	−	−	−	−	+					
Back Swamp	−	+	+	−	−					
Sand Bar	−	+	+	+	−					

Summary: *Waterfalls, rapids, wide flood plains, u-shaped valleys, meanders, and oxbows are all caused by erosion, while yazoo streams, back swamps, and sand bars are caused by deposition.*

Semantic Feature Analysis (SFA)

_____
(topic)

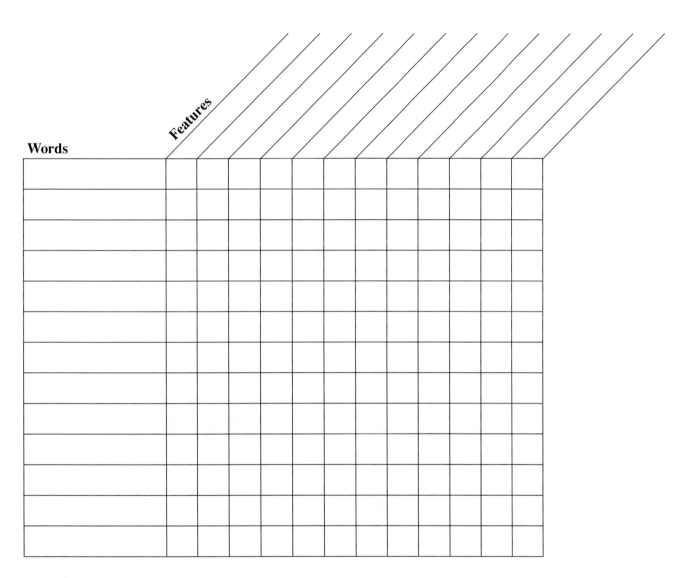

Words

Summary:

Semantic Gradient

DESCRIPTION: A Semantic Gradient (Blachowicz & Fisher, 2006) is a visual representation that depicts variations of meaning among several related words. It can help students focus on synonyms and antonyms by arranging them along a line to visually show variations in meaning. It also permits students to make connections between and among new words and concepts that they already know. Students can also use a Semantic Gradient in relation to selected words in an informational passage. Semantic Gradients are similar to linear arrays (Allen, 1999), synonym continuums (Tompkins & Blanchfield, 2004), emotion continuums (Zeigler & Johns, 2005), polar opposites, and vocabulary lines.

Focus
Vocabulary
Response

Text Type
Narrative
Informational

When to Use
After Reading

Strategy
Using Prior Knowledge
Inferring
Determining Importance
Synthesizing

How to Use
Individual
Small Group
Whole Group

Procedure

1. Draw a long line on the board. Select two words that are antonyms (like *love* and *hate*). Place one word at each end of the continuum.

   Love ——————————————————————————— Hate

   Select additional words that fit between these two extremes in meaning (for example, *care, indifferent, like, devotion, cherish, despise, crush, attracted, loathe, unconcerned, adore, detest,* and *dislike*). The specific words and the number of words used should depend on your students' maturity and the particular text being used. Write the selected words on cards for possible use later in the lesson.

2. Invite students to share information about the words at the ends of the continuum. Help students realize that the words are opposite in meaning.

3. Tell students that there are some other words whose meanings are between these two very strong emotions. Invite students to offer some words that may be related to *love* and *hate* that are not as strong. Write any words students suggest on the board.

4. You might want to model an example for students. For example, you might say the following.

   I thought of the word *indifferent*. I think I would place this word at the center of the line. Its meaning is not to care much, and that seems to be between the two words.

5. Select a word written on the board (for example, *care*) and invite students to suggest where on the line the word would best fit. Guide students as necessary and provide clarification as needed. Students should understand that the meaning of *care* is not as strong as *love*, but it is stronger than *indifferent*.

6. Continue with other words and have students discuss their meanings and place the words on the continuum. Help students realize that they are thinking about words in relation to other words. Use the words on the cards for other examples if needed.

7. Encourage students to think about ways all of these words are related. For example, you can discuss how all the words from *love* to *hate* express feelings. Help students synthesize information about the group of words on the Semantic Gradient.

8. Use a variety of continuums in subsequent lessons. For example, use weaker to stronger words or negative to positive words.

9. One variation of this strategy is to arrange the words on a ladder or steps. For example, students could be asked to arrange a group of words *(cool, hot, torrid, lukewarm, freezing, warm, boiling, scalding, chilled,* and *frigid)* from hottest to coldest. See the website for several reproducibles.

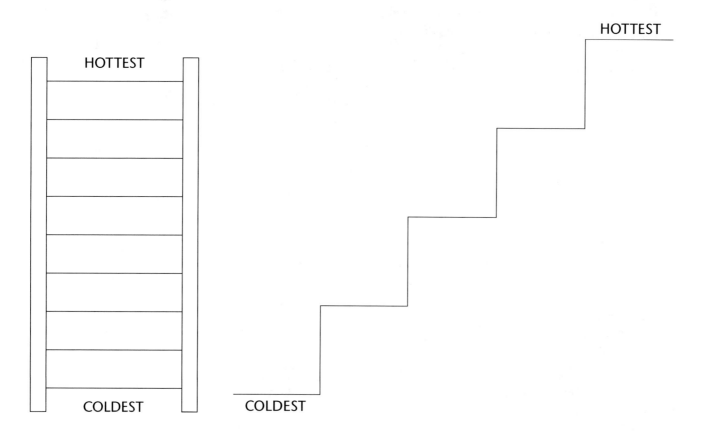

10. Another variation is to have students rate one or more character's emotions using a continuum. For example, students could think about *Romeo and Juliet* and discuss the characters' emotions. They could then rate a particular emotion. Feelings may vary at different points in the play. Below is an example for Act 1 of *Romeo and Juliet*.

Romeo   Fearful _____ x Brave
         Love x _____ Hate
         Timid _____ x Confident
         Bored _____ x Excited
         Despondent _____ x Exultant

Juliet   Love x _____ Hate
         Ignorant _____ x _____ Wise
         Eager _____ x _____ Unwilling
         Calm _____ x _____ Agitated
         Kind _____ x _____ Cruel

126

References

Allen, J. (1999). *Words, words, words: Teaching vocabulary in grades 4–12*. Portland, ME: Stenhouse.

Blachowicz, C., & Fisher, P. (2006). *Teaching vocabulary in all classrooms* (3rd ed.). Upper Saddle River, NJ: Merrill Prentice Hall.

Tompkins, G. E., & Blanchfield, C. (2004). *Teaching vocabulary.* Upper Saddle River, NJ: Merrill Prentice Hall.

Zeigler, L. L., & Johns, J. L. (2005). *Visualization: Using mental images to strengthen comprehension.* Dubuque, IA: Kendall Hunt.

SQP2RS (Squeepers)

DESCRIPTION: SQP2RS (Echevarria, Vogt, & Short, 2008; Vogt, 2000) is a framework for helping students read and study informational text. Its purpose is to teach students to read and develop cognitive and metacognitive strategies good readers use when they process text. It is especially useful for students needing modifications and support in reading textual material.

Procedure

1. **Survey.** Students are encouraged to preview the text for key concepts and to think about what they already know about the topic. Students may do this independently or with a partner using the Survey portion of the reproducible on page 131.

2. **Question.** Working with a partner or in a small group, have students develop questions they believe may be answered in the reading. Tell them they probably will not be able to answer the questions at this time, but they will have an opportunity to return to the questions and check to see if they were answered when they finish reading. When students have completed this step, invite them to share their questions with another group or with the class. Record the questions on the board and star those that are repeated by more than one group.

3. **Predict.** Students are asked to use the information from their survey, their questions, and their background knowledge to predict what they think they will learn from the text. Use the starred questions to help students develop their predictions.

4. **Read.** Students may begin reading with a partner or with their small group. This allows all students an opportunity to read the material with support. Encourage students to use sticky notes to mark sections of the text that connect to their questions and/or predictions. You may want to integrate this step with the use of Text Coding (page 141).

5. **Respond.** After the material has been read, students respond to the reading with a partner or in a small group, using the Respond section of the reproducible. Discuss any questions that weren't answered and consider additional sources of information that might be used to find the answers. The purpose of this portion of the lesson is to encourage reflection, discussion, and the development of further questions.

6. **Summarize.** Invite students to list some of the key vocabulary from the reading and use these words in their summary. After students have completed their summaries with a partner, you may wish to have students share them with the whole group. If you want to extend the learning of the key vocabulary words, incorporate the use of the Vocabulary Self-Collection Strategy on page 147.

Once students become familiar with the SQP2RS strategy, use it periodically, especially when introducing a new unit or topic of study.

Focus
Comprehension

Text Type
Informational

When to Use
Before Reading
During Reading
After Reading

Strategy
Monitoring Meaning
Using Prior Knowledge
Asking Questions
Determining Importance
Synthesizing

How to Use
Individual
Small Group
Whole Group

References

Echevarria, J., Vogt, M. E., & Short, D. J. (2008). *Making content comprehensible for English learners: The SIOP model.* Boston, MA: Pearson.

Vogt, M. E. (2000). Content learning for students needing modifications: An issue of access. In M. McLaughlin & M. E. Vogt (Eds.), *Creativity and innovation in content area teaching: A resource for intermediate, middle, and high school teachers* (pp. 329–351). Norwood, MA: Christopher Gordon.

SQP2RS (Squeepers)

Survey

Preview the text. What do you know about the topic? Look at the:

- chapter title and subtitles
- illustrations
- photos
- bold or italic type
- captions
- chapter questions

Question

With a partner, write 2 or 3 questions that you think will be answered in the reading.

1. _____

Answered?   Yes p. _____   No _____

2. _____

Answered?   Yes p. _____   No _____

3. _____

Answered?   Yes p. _____   No _____

Predict

List the important things you think you will learn from your reading.

1. _____   +   −

2. _____   +   −

3. _____   +   −

Read

Read the first section of the text. Think about your questions and predictions. Were any of the questions answered? Were your predictions confirmed?

Respond

Review the questions you wrote. Were they answered? If yes, on what pages? If no, check (✔) no.
Look at the predictions you made. Circle the plus (+) beside the ones that were confirmed. Circle the minus (−) next to the ones that were not confirmed. Discuss your ideas with your partner.

Summarize

With your partner, discuss what you learned. List the most important words from your reading. Use them to write a summary of the main ideas from the text on the back of this paper.

Sticky Notes

DESCRIPTION: Sticky Notes (Daniels & Zemelman, 2004; Harvey & Goudvis, 2000; Hoyt, 2002) encourage students to monitor their thinking while reading by jotting down brief notes and sticking them on the pages of the text that prompted their thoughts. Students can jot down brief comments, write questions, make predictions and connections, or mark an interesting phrase or sentence in the text. Sticky Notes become a record of students' thinking that can later be used for review, discussion, and assessment.

Procedure

1. Choose a passage from a text to read aloud and provide copies so that students can follow along with you. Explain that you will be stopping while reading to write down your thinking on Sticky Notes.

2. Begin reading the text aloud and stop at a point where you can share a personal connection, ask a question, make a prediction, or express appreciation of the author's use of language. For example, while reading aloud from the first chapter of *Fever 1793* (Anderson, 2000), you could stop after a mosquito bites Mattie. Ask students if they know anything about mosquitos spreading diseases. Some students may mention the West Nile Virus. Since Mattie was bitten by a mosquito, you may want to make a prediction that Mattie will become sick with yellow fever. On a Sticky Note, write down your prediction, read it aloud to students, then place it on the page to mark the spot in the text to show your thinking. Continue reading and stopping to share your written thoughts on Sticky Notes.

3. As you continue reading aloud, elicit students' thoughts. Model how to jot down their responses on the Sticky Notes using a chart, overhead transparency, or the board.

4. After modeling several examples, provide time for students to practice individually recording their thinking on Sticky Notes.

5. Invite students to share their Sticky Notes with a partner or use them in a whole class discussion. You might ask students to place their Sticky Notes on chart paper after reading a selection of text or use the reproducible on page 135. Responses can be organized into like categories and used to engage students in discussion. Possible categories might include predictions, connections, questions, visualizations, summaries, judgments, and interesting passages.

6. With informational text, you can demonstrate how to mark a photo or illustration in the text with a question. Students can be encouraged to record their senses to help comprehend text. For example, while reading an article in National Geographic titled "Thailand's Urban Giants," students could be asked to write what they saw, heard, smelled, tasted, and felt about the inhumane treatment of the elephants.

7. Upon completion of the reading, students should have a collection of Sticky Notes that can be stored in a notebook for later discussion and review.

8. Another reproducible for possible use can be found on the website.

Focus
Comprehension
Response

Text Type
Narrative
Informational

When to Use
During Reading
After Reading

Strategy
Monitoring Meaning
Using Prior Knowledge
Asking Questions
Creating Images
Determining Importance
Synthesizing

How to Use
Individual

References

Anderson, H. L. (2000). *Fever 1793*. New York, NY: Aladdin.

Daniels, H., & Zemelman, S. (2004). *Subjects matter: Every teacher's guide to content-area reading.* Portsmouth, NH: Heinemann.

Harvey, S., & Goudvis, A. (2000). *Strategies that work.* Portland, ME: Stenhouse.

Hoyt, L. (2002). *Make it real: Strategies for success with informational texts.* Portsmouth, NH: Heinemann.

Sticky Notes Record Sheet

Title _____

My Predictions	My Images
My Connections	**My Questions**
My Summary	**My Evaluation**

Story Map

Focus
Comprehension

Text Type
Narrative

When to Use
After Reading

Strategy
Asking Questions
Inferring
Determining Importance
Synthesizing

How to Use
Individual
Small Group

DESCRIPTION: Story mapping (Beck & McKeown, 1981) provides a graphic representation of a story or novel by displaying the key story elements. By completing a Story Map and identifying the plot, characters, setting, problem, resolution, and theme, students can demonstrate their comprehension of the common elements of a story and create a visual aid to enable them to better remember a story (Buehl, 2009). Two types of Story Map reproducible masters are provided: one on page 139 and one on the website.

Procedure

1. Select two short stories that clearly illustrate the common story elements such as plot, characters, setting, problem, resolution, and theme. One story will be for you to model the strategy to students and the other story will be for students to read and map on their own. There is an example of a completed Story Map on page 138.

2. Read the story to the class that you will use to model the Story Map strategy.

3. Display and duplicate copies of one of the Story Map reproducible masters or adapt it to suit your needs or purposes.

4. Model for students how to complete a Story Map. Discuss with students the basic outline of the story in terms of its common elements. As students describe the plot, characters, setting, problem, solution, and theme, you could model how to simplify their descriptions and write them in the appropriate places on the map. You may need to restate students' descriptions to simplify them. If so, think aloud how to keep the descriptions brief and concise. For example, if a student described the setting of the sample story "Mr. Diskin" in a long paragraph, such as, "The story takes place in the town of Jonesville, USA. The two main settings are in the Diskins' house and in the dollar store that's downtown," you would model the appropriateness of writing in short phrases instead. For example, "Jonesville, USA; the Diskins' house; the downtown dollar store."

5. Reproduce and distribute copies of the Story Map on page 139 and the second short story. Explain to students that they are to first read the story and then complete the Story Map. Assure them that it is appropriate to go back and reread parts of the story to help them identify the common elements.

6. When students are finished completing the Story Maps on their own, ask them to share their Story Maps in small groups. Have them discuss how decisions were made and provide opportunities for students to explain why they agree or disagree with one another's Story Map descriptions. For example, in a story about a boy drowning in a river, one student may say that the river can be considered to be a character and another student may disagree. In a story about Holocaust survivors, one student may see a theme of the strength of family love and another student may see a theme of persecution.

7. Give students opportunities to design their own Story Maps to reflect the nature of the stories they are reading. For example, students reading a story about ancient Egypt may wish to create a Story Map in the shape of a pyramid. Students reading a story about a haunted house may wish to create a Story Map in the shape of a house.

8. As an extension activity, discuss with students how they may use Story Maps to help them organize their own writing.

References

Beck, I., & McKeown, M. (1981). Developing questions that promote comprehension: The story map. *Language Arts, 58,* 913–918.

Buehl, D. (2009). *Classroom strategies for interactive learning* (3rd ed.). Newark, DE: International Reading Association.

Sample Story Map for Middle School **Literature**

Title
Mr. Diskin

Setting
Jonesville, USA; the Diskin's house; the downtown dollar store

---

Characters
Mr. Diskin, Mrs. Diskin, their daughter Irma, and the owner of the downtown dollar store

---

Problem
Irma wants to be treated like a grown up, but she is only 13.

Events

Irma lies about her age to get a job at the downtown dollar store.

↓

Mr. & Mrs. Diskin wonder why Irma suddenly has so much money.
They are worried and curious.

↓

Irma hears her parents talking and has to decide whether to tell her boss and her parents the truth.

↓

When Mrs. Diskin goes shopping, she goes to the store Irma is working in and finds out the truth before Irma has chance to tell her.

Solution   *Irma apologizes to her boss and her parents for lying and explains she wanted to feel more grown up. Her boss hires her to babysit, and her parents decide not to ground her.*

Story Map

Title

Setting

Characters

Problem

Events

↓

↓

↓

Solution

Text Coding

DESCRIPTION: Good readers conduct active conversations in their heads by reacting to, questioning, and synthesizing information as they read. All readers can be helped to become more aware of their thinking and engaged in the reading process. One method for doing so is through the use of Text Coding (Harvey & Goudvis, 2007; Tovani, 2000; Vaughn & Estes, 1986). Using a simple coding system, students make notations in the margins of the text or on sticky notes, encouraging them to monitor their comprehension as they read. Text Codes can increase in number and complexity depending on students' maturity, comfort, and experience in using them. By using Text Codes, students think critically as they read the assigned material and are more prepared to discuss their thoughts and reactions with others.

Procedure

1. Select reading material and display it for students to see.

2. Read a portion of the text aloud, modeling how proficient readers carry on internal conversations in their heads as they read. Highlight, underline, or make comments on the displayed text reflecting your thoughts.

3. After modeling several think-alouds for students, introduce a few simple Text Codes. Show how underlining and highlighting can be replaced with a marginal notation or sticky note containing a * (very important information; key concept; new information), a ? (confusing information; something doesn't make sense; question), a ✔ (something you already knew), or a ! (Wow! Something you find interesting, hard to believe, or unexpected).

4. Provide students with text material that can be written on or give them small sticky notes to use for their codes. Invite students to read the text and use the codes to track their thinking. You may wish to provide copies of the reproducible on page 142 and have students highlight specific codes that you want them to use. Start with a small number and increase as needed.

5. After students have coded the text, invite them to discuss their reactions with a partner.

6. As students become more experienced with coding their thinking as they read, form discussion groups of five or six students. Select a discussion leader to compose questions for the group to discuss. Each student in the group is responsible to prepare their Text Coding as evidence that they have thought critically about their reading.

7. When the groups come together, the discussion leader facilitates the conversation about the text and all students participate, using their coded material as the basis for their comments.

References

Harvey, S., & Goudvis, A. (2007). *Strategies that work: Teaching comprehension for understanding and engagement* (2nd ed.). Portland, ME: Stenhouse.

Tovani, C. (2000). *I read it, but I don't get it: Comprehension strategies for adolescent readers.* Portland, ME: Stenhouse.

Vaughn, J. L., & Estes, T. H. (1986). *Reading and reasoning beyond the primary grades.* Boston: Allyn & Bacon.

Focus
Comprehension

Text Type
Narrative
Informational

When to Use
During Reading
After Reading

Strategy
Monitoring Meaning
Using Prior Knowledge
Asking Questions
Inferring
Creating Images
Determining Importance
Synthesizing

How to Use
Individual
Small Group

Text Codes

Code Symbol	Meaning
*	Very important information; key concept; new information
?	Confusing information; something doesn't make sense; question
!	Wow! Something you find interesting, hard to believe, or unexpected
✓	Something you already knew
V	Something you can visualize; make a picture in your mind
P	You can make a prediction
2 + 2	You put ideas together (synthesize)
X	Something you disagree with or that contradicts what you thought
R	Reminds you of something
T-S	Text-to-Self connection
T-T	Text-to-Text connection
T-W	Text-to-World connection
C	Connects to something you know about
A	Something you agree with

Text Codes

Code Symbol	Meaning
*	Very important information; key concept; new information
?	Confusing information; something doesn't make sense; question
!	Wow! Something you find interesting, hard to believe, or unexpected
✓	Something you already knew
V	Something you can visualize; make a picture in your mind
P	You can make a prediction
2 + 2	You put ideas together (synthesize)
X	Something you disagree with or that contradicts what you thought
R	Reminds you of something
T-S	Text-to-Self connection
T-T	Text-to-Text connection
T-W	Text-to-World connection
C	Connects to something you know about
A	Something you agree with

Text Dialogue

DESCRIPTION: The purpose of Text Dialogue (Lenski, Wham, Johns, & Caskey, 2011) is to help students process and reflect on what they have read by summarizing, interpreting, and evaluating. Students complete the Text Dialogue after reading and then interact with their peers and teacher to further discuss the reading. Instead of requiring comprehension questions to be answered or book reports to be written following a reading assignment, the Text Dialogue strategy may be assigned as an alternate means of demonstrating comprehension. This strategy is an adaptation of the Book Dialogue strategy, created by Miller (1994) as a tool for students in a college developmental reading course to improve their skills of reflection and response.

Procedure

1. Display and duplicate copies of the Text Dialogue reproducible master on page 145. You may wish to adapt it to suit your needs or purposes.

2. Choose text selections that students will be asked to read. Choose one passage from the text to use for modeling the strategy and choose another passage for independent student practice.

3. Use the sample Text Dialogue on page 144 to demonstrate for students how the strategy works. Model for them how to complete the sheet. First, complete the information at the top of the form, and then think aloud as you write a summary of the most important ideas. Next, think aloud as you write your own interpretation of the passage. Stress to students that their well-thought-out reasoning is more important than trying to find the "right" answer. Finally, think aloud as you evaluate the reading. Address critical issues such as accuracy, your level of interest, whether the style of writing is engaging, and the likelihood that you would seek out either more information on this topic or more literature by this author. In this final step, emphasize to students that it is their opportunity to be the critics. Explain that it is important for students to support their opinions with specific reasons.

4. Distribute blank copies of the Text Dialogue reproducible on page 145, instruct students to read the selected passage, and have them complete the form after they have finished reading.

5. Assign each student a partner. Instruct the partners to discuss their text dialogues in the context of the following guiding questions:
   - In what areas did you and your partner disagree? Why?
   - What specific examples can you use to support your opinions?
   - How were your and your partner's interpretations similar and different?
   - How were your and your partner's evaluations similar and different?
   - How did making connections help you understand the material?

   Suggest that the partners keep notes of the outcome of their discussion so that they will be prepared to share their comments with the class.

6. Once the partners have finished their discussions, bring the whole class together to share their thoughts.

Focus
Comprehension
Response

Text Type
Narrative

When to Use
After Reading

Strategy
Using Prior Knowledge
Asking Questions
Inferring
Determining Importance
Synthesizing

How to Use
Individual
Small Group

References

Lenski, S. D., Wham, M. A., Johns, J. L., & Caskey, M. M. (2011). *Reading and learning strategies: Middle grades through high school* (4th ed.). Dubuque, IA: Kendall Hunt.

Miller, E. F. (1994). Book dialogues. *Journal of Reading, 37,* 415–416.

Sample Text Dialogue for High School **Literature**

Title: *Awesome Women*

Author: *A. Love-Green*

Type of Text: *Biography*

What I thought was most important:

> *Throughout history, there have been strong, smart, independent women who were persecuted because they were different. Some were young, some were old, some were rich, some were poor. They all were punished for their strengths. Even today, some women are under suspicion because they don't fit society's ideas of how women should look, think, act, and live.*

My interpretation:

> *This means to me that it is okay to be different and that I should not be so quick to decide that I do not like someone just because she acts or looks differently from me. If more women had the courage to be themselves, and if people weren't so judgmental, the world would be a better place.*

What it meant to me:

> *This text was very meaningful to me because I like to read about good female role models. I could tell that Love-Green really worked hard to find accurate information about the women in her book. It was helpful because it gave me ideas of women to write about the next time I have to do a research paper.*

Text Dialogue

Title: _____

Author: _____

Type of Text: _____

What I thought was most important:

```
┌──────────────────────────────────────────────────────────────────────┐
│                                                                        │
│                                                                        │
│                                                                        │
│                                                                        │
│                                                                        │
│                                                                        │
└──────────────────────────────────────────────────────────────────────┘
```

My interpretation:

```
┌──────────────────────────────────────────────────────────────────────┐
│                                                                        │
│                                                                        │
│                                                                        │
│                                                                        │
│                                                                        │
│                                                                        │
└──────────────────────────────────────────────────────────────────────┘
```

What it meant to me:

```
┌──────────────────────────────────────────────────────────────────────┐
│                                                                        │
│                                                                        │
│                                                                        │
│                                                                        │
│                                                                        │
│                                                                        │
└──────────────────────────────────────────────────────────────────────┘
```

Vocabulary Self-Collection Strategy (VSS)

Focus
Vocabulary

Text Type
Narrative
Informational

When to Use
Before Reading
After Reading

Strategy
Inferring
Determining Importance

How to Use
Small Group
Whole Group

DESCRIPTION: The Vocabulary Self-Collection Strategy (Haggard, 1986; Ruddell & Shearer, 2002) is a simple, powerful technique to help promote long term vocabulary growth in all content areas. Central to the strategy is the self-selection of words to be learned. Students identify possible vocabulary in reading assignments to explore and learn through conversations with other students and the entire class. The strategy generates an interest in words that can help strengthen vocabulary growth.

Procedure

1. Display the Vocabulary Self-Collection Strategy (VSS) reproducible on page 149 to help introduce the VSS. You may also want to make copies of page 149 for each student.

2. Model each of the areas by saying the following.

   I have reviewed the assignment you are about to read, and I would like to nominate one word that I think we should learn. The word is labor force. It is found on page 95 in this sentence: The United States labor force totaled 127 million in 1992 and is expected to reach over 160 million in 2013. [Write the appropriate information on the transparency.] I looked the word up in the glossary and found it meant the number of people over the age of 16 who are actively seeking work. I found the meaning in the glossary, so I will check glossary on the form. The word is important to learn for at least two reasons. First, the assignment deals with jobs of the future and what the labor force will look like. Second, the text shares information about how the labor force will be changing by the time many of you are making career choices. You will now be asked to use the sheet I've shared to nominate a word that our class should learn.

3. Divide the class into groups of two to five students.

4. Have students go through the reading assignment and identify one word they believe the entire class should learn. The word should be important in the reading selection. The reproducible on page 149 will help guide students through the process. As students work, circulate among the groups to offer encouragement and assistance as needed. Each group should decide which word to select and note the page and paragraph where it is found. They should then write the sentence containing the word, determine its meaning, and generate reasons why the word should be learned. Provide sufficient time for students to complete the sheet for the nominated word.

5. Call the groups together and have them present their nominated word to the entire class. One person from each group

   - identifies the word and reads the sentence in which the word is used.

   - offers the group's consensus regarding the meaning of the word.

   - provides reasons why the word is important enough for the class to learn.

6. As each group shares, facilitate the discussion, write the nominated words on the board with consensus meanings, and encourage additional clarifications of the words as needed.

7. After all words are presented, the class should eliminate duplications, words already known, and words students do not want to learn.

8. The resulting words and their definitions can be written on the reproducible found on page 150—Words Chosen for Vocabulary Self-Collection. The resulting list "focuses on words that students want to learn, that are important to them, and about which they have expressed interest and curiosity" (Ruddell & Shearer, 2002, p. 353).

9. Facilitate further learning in subsequent class sessions through discussion, Semantic Mapping (see page 75), Semantic Feature Analysis (see page 121), Concept Circles (see page 17), and other interactive word activities.

10. The reproducible on the website can be used by individual students to develop their unique vocabulary notebooks.

References

Haggard, M. R. (1986). The vocabulary self-collection strategy: Using student interest and world knowledge to enhance vocabulary growth. *Journal of Reading, 29*, 634–642.

Ruddell, M. R., & Shearer, B. A. (2002). "Extraordinary," "tremendous," "exhilarating," "magnificent": Middle school at-risk students become avid word learners with the Vocabulary Self-Collection Strategy (VSS). *Journal of Adolescent & Adult Literacy, 45*, 352–363.

Vocabulary Self-Collection Strategy (VSS)

Names of Group Members _____

Title of Selection or Text _____

Word Selected _____ Page/Paragraph _____

Word in Sentence _____

What does the word mean?

_____

_____

_____

_____

We used _____ Context

  _____ Glossary

  _____ Dictionary

  _____ Other

Why we think the word is important to learn.

_____

_____

_____

_____

_____

_____

_____

Words Chosen for Vocabulary Self-Collection

Title of Text or Selection _____

Pages _____

Word	**Meaning**
1. _____	_____
	_____
	_____
2. _____	_____
	_____
	_____
3. _____	_____
	_____
	_____
4. _____	_____
	_____
	_____
5. _____	_____
	_____
	_____
6. _____	_____
	_____
	_____
7. _____	_____
	_____
	_____
8. _____	_____
	_____
	_____

Word Map

Focus
Vocabulary

Text Type
Narrative
Informational

When to Use
During Reading
After Reading

Strategy
Determining Importance

How to Use
Individual
Small Group

DESCRIPTION: A Word Map (Schwartz & Raphael, 1985) is a graphic representation of the definition of a word. The map contains the word, the category to which it belongs, some of its essential characteristics, and some examples. These elements compose a good definition. Word Maps help students understand the attributes and characteristics of a word's meaning. A Word Map engages students to go beyond a word's definition as suggested by Beck, McKeown, and Kucan (2002). Due to the time it takes to complete the map, the Word Map graphic organizer should be used for key concept words. It is most effectively used with nouns.

Procedure

1. Display the Word Map graphic organizer on page 153. Tell students that this type of map can help them think about what they need to know in order to understand a new word.

2. Model the use of the map by choosing a well-understood concept and inviting the class to participate in completing the map with you. For example, the chosen word might be *ice cream*. Write *ice cream* in the box in the center. Ask, "What is it?" Students might say, "food" or "dessert." Write one of the responses in the proper place. Then ask, "What makes ice cream different from other foods or dairy products?" Properties might include *frozen, sweet, creamy, melts*. List these properties in the proper place. Finally, ask students for some kinds of ice cream they know. Examples could be *chocolate, strawberry*, and *vanilla*. Write these words in the appropriate place.

3. Duplicate the Word Map reproducible master on page 153 and distribute copies to students.

4. Present a key term or concept from the lesson.

5. Invite students to work individually or in pairs to complete a map for the key concept word. They may wish to use their textbooks, their own background knowledge, or a combination of resources to assist them.

6. When the maps are completed, have students share some of their ideas and then write a definition of the key concept word. The definition should include the category of the word, some properties or characteristics, and specific examples. For instance, the definition of ice cream might be, "Ice cream is a dessert that is frozen, tastes sweet, is creamy, and melts if it is left at room temperature or when it is eaten. Chocolate, strawberry, and vanilla are three popular kinds of ice cream."

7. An example of a Word Map for algebra is on the next page. Additional Word Maps and an example can be found on the website.

References

Beck, I. L., McKeown, M. G., & Kucan, L. (2002). *Bringing words to life: Robust vocabulary instruction*. New York: Guilford.

Schwartz, R. M., & Raphael, T. E. (1985). Concept of definition: A key to improving students' vocabulary. *The Reading Teacher, 39*, 198–205.

Sample Word Map for **Algebra**

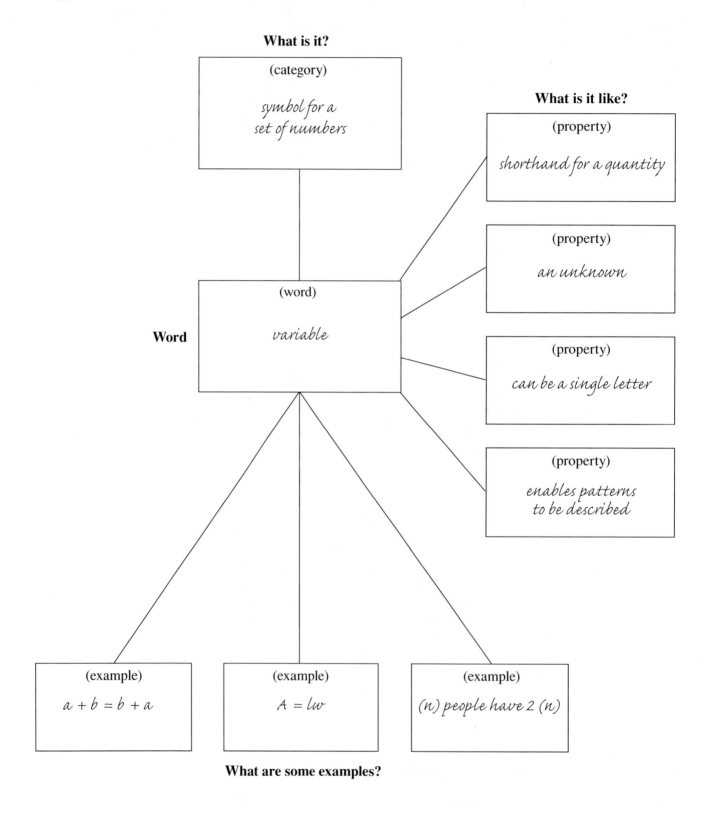

What is it?

(category)

symbol for a set of numbers

What is it like?

(property)

shorthand for a quantity

(property)

an unknown

(property)

can be a single letter

(property)

enables patterns to be described

Word

(word)

variable

(example)

$a + b = b + a$

(example)

$A = lw$

(example)

(n) people have 2 (n)

What are some examples?

Word Map

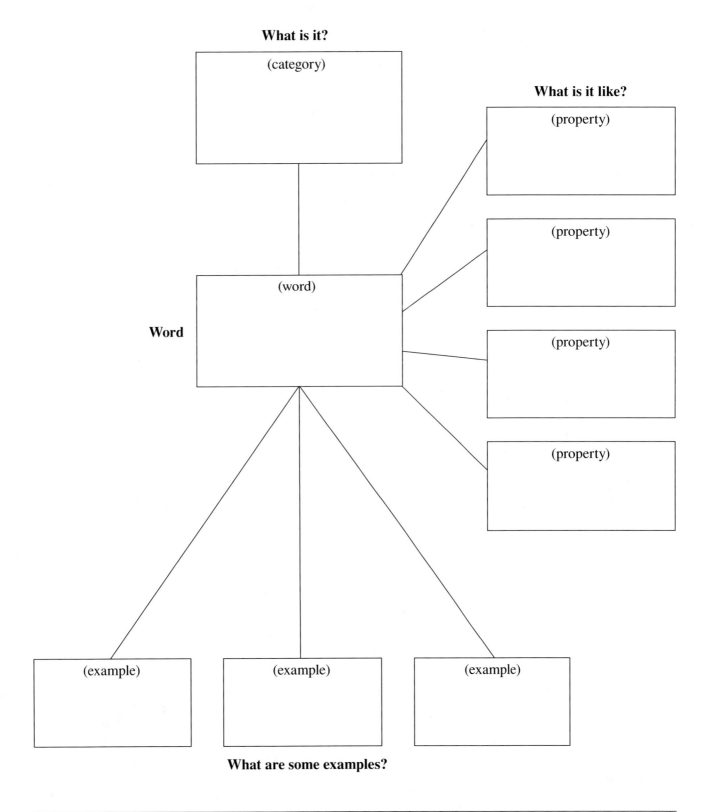

What is it?

(category)

What is it like?

(property)

(property)

(property)

(property)

Word

(word)

(example)

(example)

(example)

What are some examples?

Word Sort

Focus
Vocabulary
Comprehension

Text Type
Informational

When to Use
Before Reading
After Reading

Strategy
Asking Questions
Inferring
Determining Importance
Synthesizing

How to Use
Small Group

DESCRIPTION: In a Word Sort (Gillet & Kita, 1979), students classify words into categories based on their prior knowledge and experiences. The Word Sort strategy is derived from Taba's (1967) List-Group-Label strategy and is based on the belief that placing words into categories helps students to organize and remember vocabulary and concepts. There are two types of Word Sorts, open and closed. In a Closed Word Sort, the categories are predetermined. Closed Word Sorts are generally easier for students because all of the words are clustered under the selected headings that are given to them. In an Open Word Sort, students are invited to consider characteristics and meanings of the words and then cluster the words into categories that they select. Some of the words in the sort can be used for category headings, or students can create new headings. Word Sorts can be used before reading to elicit background knowledge and set purposes for reading or as an after-reading activity to consolidate and refine new learning. Inviting students to sort the same words both before and after reading encourages reflection and refinement of the major concepts in the lesson. This sorting provides a cross-checking experience that can enhance metacognition (awareness of one's own learning).

Procedure

1. Select 15–20 vocabulary words that are important for understanding the lesson. Be sure to include some familiar words along with the new words students will be encountering.

2. Write the words on note cards. Make identical sets of cards for each small group. (An alternate idea is to write the words on the reproducible master on page 157 and have students cut them apart for sorting.)

3. Cluster students into groups of 3–5 students, giving each group a set of the note cards containing the vocabulary words.

4. If it is a Closed Word Sort, inform the students of the categories that you have selected. If it is an Open Word Sort, tell the students to read the words and cluster them into categories that make sense to them. They need to be able to defend their classifications.

5. Allow students about ten minutes to complete the sort. After students have completed the Word Sort, invite groups to rotate around the classroom, examining how others have clustered the words, or have them share their classifications orally.

6. As students read or experience the lesson, direct them to reclassify their words based on their expanding knowledge of the subject area.

7. Invite students to share their reflections. Were their initial classifications correct? Did they make changes? If so, why?

References

Gillet, J., & Kita, M. J. (1979). Words, kids and categories. *The Reading Teacher, 32,* 538–542.

Taba, H. (1967). *Teacher's handbook for elementary social studies.* Reading, MA: Addison-Wesley.

Sample Open Word Sort for Middle School *Science*

Directions: Below are some words that you will find in your lesson. Cut them apart and arrange them in categories according to their meanings. You must be able to justify the reasons for your decisions.

$$\frac{\text{The Sun}}{\text{(topic)}}$$

solar flare	solar composition	magnetic storm
solar structure	helium	photosphere
aurora	core	solar wind
atmosphere	hydrogen	sunspot
corona	prominence	chromosphere
solar activities	solar eclipse	nuclear fusion

Sample Closed Word Sort for Intermediate Grade *Social Studies*

Directions: Arrange each of the words below into one of the categories in bold type.

$$\frac{\text{Anasazi Indians}}{\text{(topic)}}$$

Who They Were		**What They Did**		**Where They Lived**
ancient ones	nomadic	canyon	invaders	cliff palace
kiva	metates	abode	cliffs	stone masons
hunters	mesa	excavation	swallows	preserve

Word Sort

_____
(topic)

Directions: Below are some words that you will find in your lesson. Cut them apart and arrange them in categories according to their meanings. You must be able to justify the reasons for your decisions.
